THE DESIGNER'S TOOLKIT 1000 COLORS

THOUSANDS OF COLOR COMBINATIONS

THE DESIGNER'S TOOLKIT 1000 COLORS
THOUSANDS OF COLOR COMBINATIONS

Graham Davis

CHRONICLE BOOKS

SAN FRANCISCO

Library of Congress Cataloging-in-Publication Data
available.

ISBN: 978-0-8118-6305-6

Manufactured in China.

10 9 8 7 6 5 4 3 2 1

Chronicle Books LLC
680 Second Street
San Francisco, CA 94107

www.chroniclebooks.com

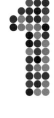

CONTENTS

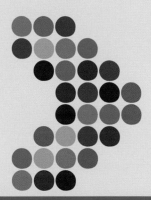

Introduction:
How to use this book

Color is fundamental to all design. It can be used to evoke a mood, to grab attention, to identify a product, or to organize information. In the pre-digital age the choice of color was limited by the availability of pigments, but no such constraint exists today. With at least 16 million different colors to choose from, the problem for today's digital artist and designer is how to narrow down the options. Step forward the book in your hands. This title, and its all-important CD, contains specially selected color palettes that are an invaluable tool for designers, architects, decorators, and anyone involved in selecting, applying, and specifying color.

We live in a world saturated by color. It is brought into our homes by the media, we are assaulted by it in every store and shopping mall, but it was not always so. For our grandparents it was very different. When they purchased an automobile they could have any color so long as it was black. They watched their favorite football team on a black-and-white TV. Their glossy magazines were mainly black-and-white, the shelves in the hardware store had only a handful of different paint colors and their clothes were drab and monotonous.

But if you travel back a little further, to the Victorian and Edwardian eras, color had been at the forefront, particularly in packaging and poster art. But it was the increasing dominance of photography over illustration that resulted in this long period in the monochromatic doldrums. In fact, it was not until color photography began to replace black-and-white that things began to change. It is no coincidence that the explosion of color in all aspects of design and fashion that began in the 1960s was associated with advances in color photography and printing, color reproduction, and color in broadcasting.

The effectiveness of color in both organizing information and selling goods had always been recognized. For hundreds of years atlas publishers used color to separate boundaries and to identify features like rivers and height levels. In the 1930s there appeared one of the most iconic examples of color and design, the London Underground map. The brainchild of Harry Beck, his design concept and color coding has been copied by just about every mass transit system in the world.

The great corporations also recognized the power of color and made strenuous efforts to associate their businesses with particular colors; Kodak with yellow, McDonald's with red & gold, and IBM blue, to the extent that IBM was known colloquially as "Big Blue." Color had become an integral part of every company's corporate identity and huge sums were spent to develop and protect a company's image and the brands it owned (it is now possible to trademark a color).

Color associations extended into politics and the wider world, the communist era in the former Soviet Union and China associated with red, and the environmental and conservation campaigns with green.

Today we are spoiled for choice. Even the most modest computer includes tools that the professional of twenty-five years ago could only have dreamt of. We can see almost any color on screen, we can print it out cheaply and accurately on our desktop printer, or send it electronically to just about any device, anywhere in the world.

Color is, and always will be, an enormously powerful part of human experience and therefore one of the most potent tools available to the designer and artist as, like music, it can play directly on the emotions. It has fascinated scientists and psychologists, as well as artists, and numerous theories exist to explain how we perceive color, why color combinations clash or are harmonious, and why particular colors—like red for danger—have developed an association.

This book is intended as a tool for those of us who use color in our work. It should save valuable time, and perhaps it will also inspire you to start collecting your own color palettes, just as artists have done in times past.

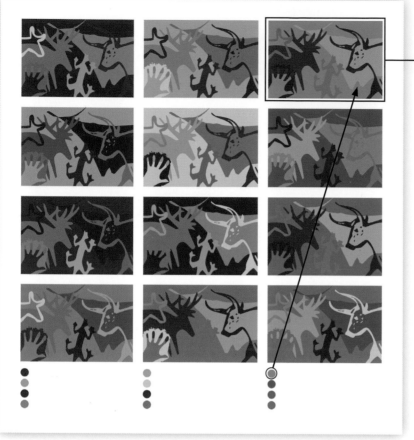

The background color of a template normally corresponds with the three columns of dots below. In this example, from a palette of twelve colors, seven have been used in each template graphic.

The appearance of a color will always be affected by adjacent colors, so this book employs a series of thumbnail graphics to show how a palette of colors will appear in a variety of twelve juxtapositions. Beneath the templates is a key that shows the *CMYK, RGB,* and *Hexadecimal* values of each color, while on the accompanying CD each palette has been saved in a variety of industry standard formats (see box, facing page) so that the palette can be reused or converted to other color measuring or describing systems.

This book is structured by color themes, inspired by an historical period, a psychological mood, the natural world, and more, enabling designers to quickly find color combinations that work for a particular project. The palettes usually contain twelve colors and by using the files on the CD you can, for example, load a palette directly into an *Adobe Creative Suite (CS)* application by selecting the *Adobe Swatch Exchange* format. For Quark users with version 4.1 or later a *Quark 4 Library File*

(.qxl) is also included. If you are a Web designer you can open a .png version of the palette and sample the colors using the eyedropper tool, or type the *Hexadecimal* value shown in the key directly into an application like *Dreamweaver* or into *HTML* or *CSS* code. For architects and interior designers it is probably best to use the color match scanners used by all paint suppliers to convert to specific paint mixes.

As well as the palettes, each set of twelve template graphics is also included on the CD, just as they appear in the book.

The template pages are interspersed with *Color at Work* spreads. In each case, four of the palette templates have been selected to show how the color combinations might be used in a real-life situation. In most examples the text is rendered in one of the template colors, but where text is shown in black or white this is in addition to the template color set. For the graphic designer, color is rarely used in isolation but is invariably combined with images. A pale, low-key image may be

The *Color at Work* spreads that follow some of the palette templates demonstrate how a palette can be used in a real-life situation. In this example, the Art Deco–inspired color set has been used in a pastiche layout that references a well-known travel poster illustration of the period. The text also appears in the palette livery, but is still quite legible, despite the relatively small font size.

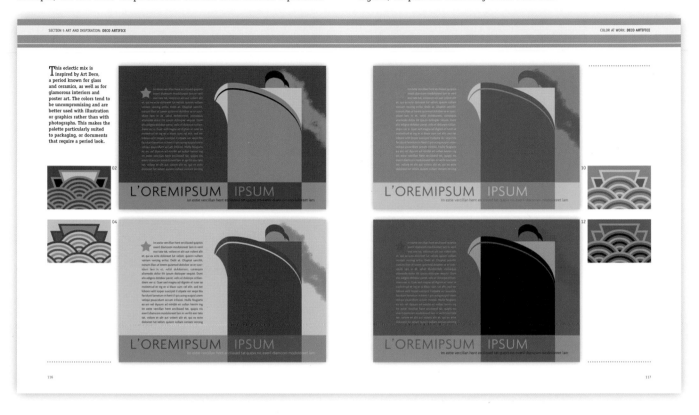

overwhelmed by intense, contrasting colors, while a powerful image may look out of place against a series of pastel colors. So it is important to consider all of the elements in a design before choosing a palette.

Despite its many advantages, the advent of digital color has introduced the anomaly of *RGB* and *CMYK* color gamuts that can make conversions from *RGB* to *CMYK* problematic. There are a range of colors that are visible on a computer screen *(Red, Green, and Blue)* that cannot be printed (using *Cyan, Magenta, Yellow, and Key/Black)*. Even using additional spot colors, many of these are still out of range. To overcome this, all the colors used here will be constant whether reproduced in *RGB* or *CMYK*.

To get the best from this book, and the CD, it is important that your computer monitor is set up correctly. Always follow the manufacturer's instructions, along with those of the operating system, plus any that are specific to the software that you are using, for example *Adobe Gamma*.

On the CD
The color palettes shown on the template spreads are saved on the CD in the following formats.

Saved in Adobe Swatch Exchange format (.ase)*
Saved as CMYK TIFFs
Saved as RGB TIFFs
Saved as RGB PNGs
Saved as Quark 4 Libraries (.qxl)
Each template page is also saved as CMYK TIFF
Each template page is also saved as RGB TIFF

* Adobe Swatch Exchange is RGB, but when loaded (in Photoshop) it shows CMYK and Hexadecimal values as well in the Color Picker as well.

Atmospherics and Location

01
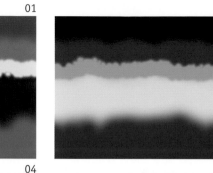

02
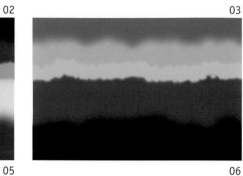

03

04

05
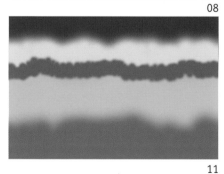

06

07

08
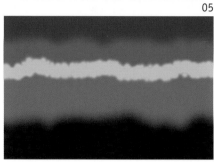

09
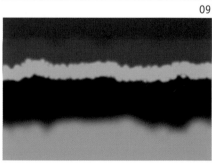

10
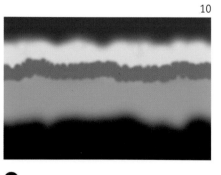

11
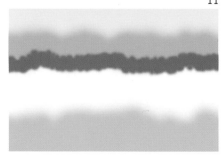

12
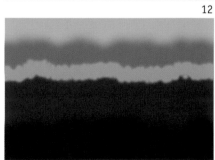

- C083 M078 Y049 K053 / R031 G032 B045 / #1E202D
- C080 M024 Y012 K000 / R175 G175 B193 / #AFAFC1
- C065 M056 Y022 K002 / R090 G092 B130 / #5A5C82
- C051 M022 Y011 K000 / R119 G159 B190 / #779FBE

- C014 M019 Y004 K000 / R218 G220 B231 / #DADCE7
- C057 M049 Y035 K007 / R103 G103 B115 / #676773
- C027 M017 Y002 K000 / R183 G193 B220 / #B7C1DC
- C008 M001 Y000 K000 / R248 G250 B252 / #F8FAFC

- C080 M074 Y050 K005 / R059 G060 B078 / #3B3C4E
- C009 M007 Y001 K000 / R229 G230 B241 / #E5E6F1
- C082 M076 Y058 K077 / R018 G019 B024 / #121318
- C095 M073 Y035 K020 / R010 G051 B083 / #0A3353

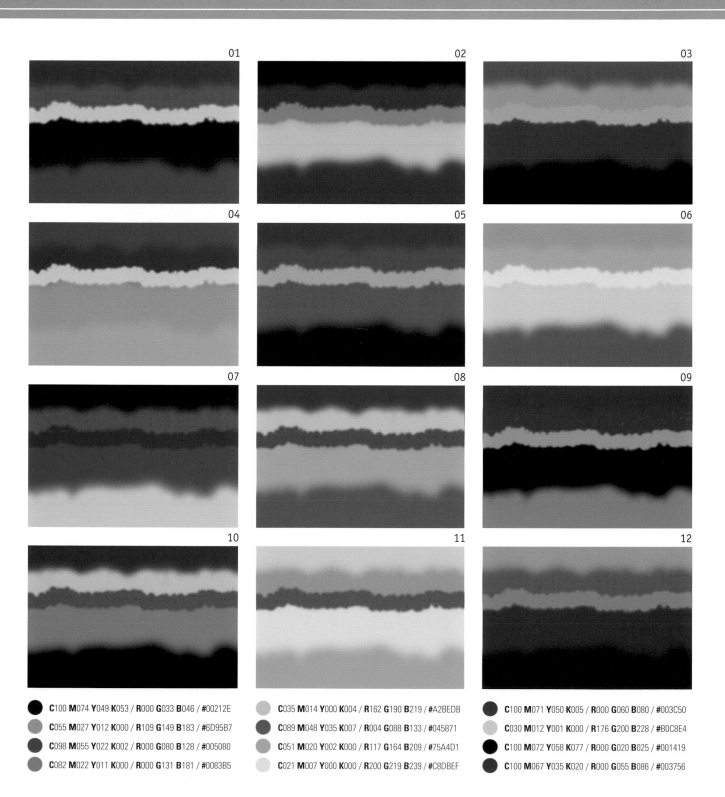

C100 **M**074 **Y**049 **K**053 / **R**000 **G**033 **B**046 / #00212E

C055 **M**027 **Y**012 **K**000 / **R**109 **G**149 **B**183 / #6D95B7

C098 **M**055 **Y**022 **K**002 / **R**000 **G**080 **B**128 / #005080

C082 **M**022 **Y**011 **K**000 / **R**000 **G**131 **B**181 / #0083B5

C035 **M**014 **Y**000 **K**004 / **R**162 **G**190 **B**219 / #A2BEDB

C089 **M**048 **Y**035 **K**007 / **R**004 **G**088 **B**133 / #045871

C051 **M**020 **Y**002 **K**000 / **R**117 **G**164 **B**209 / #75A4D1

C021 **M**007 **Y**000 **K**000 / **R**200 **G**219 **B**239 / #C8DBEF

C100 **M**071 **Y**050 **K**005 / **R**000 **G**060 **B**080 / #003C50

C030 **M**012 **Y**001 **K**000 / **R**176 **G**200 **B**228 / #B0C8E4

C100 **M**072 **Y**058 **K**077 / **R**000 **G**020 **B**025 / #001419

C100 **M**067 **Y**035 **K**020 / **R**000 **G**055 **B**086 / #003756

This twelve-color palette inspired by moonlight uses dark blues and near blacks with two pale blues that derive from the colors found around the edges of clouds when illuminated by the moon. It is suited to projects with small amounts of text as much of it will have to be dropped out of a dark background. Here it is used in a program for a modern interpretation of a classical composer.

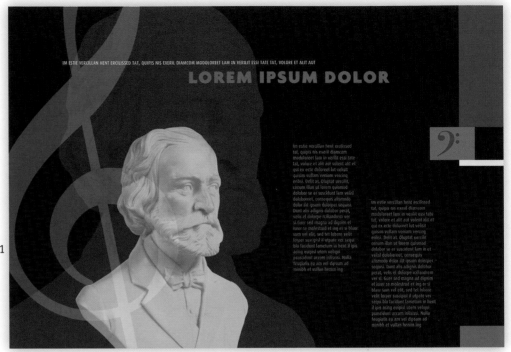

LOREM IPSUM DOLOR

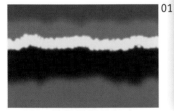
01

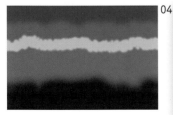
04

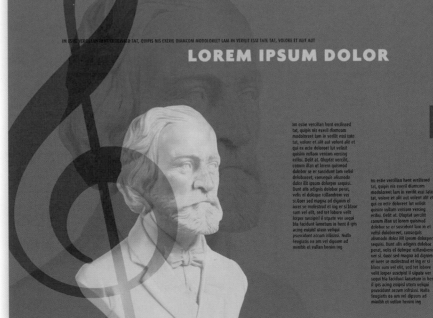

LOREM IPSUM DOLOR

LOREM IPSUM DOLOR

IM ESTIE VERCILLAN HENT ERCILISSED TAT, QUIPIS NIS EXERIL DIAMCOM MODOLOREET LAM IN VERILIT ESSI TATE TAT, VOLORE ET ALIT AUT

Im estie vercillan hent ercilissed tat, quipis nis exeril diamcom modoloreet lam in verilit essi tate tat, volore et alit aut volent alit et qui ex ecte doloreet lut velisit quisim vullam veniam vercing erilisi. Delit at. Oluptat uercilit, conum illan ut lorem quismod dolobor se er suscidunt lam velisl doloboreet, consequis alismodo dolor ilit ipsum dolorper sequisi. Dunt olis adignis dolobor perat, velis el dolorpe rcillandrem ver si.Guer sed magna ad dignim el iurer se molestrud et ing er si blaor sum vel elit, sed tet lobore velit lorper suscipisl il utpate ver sequi bla facidunt lametum in hent il ipis acing euipisl utem veliqui psuscidunt accum irilisissi. Nulla feugiatis ea am vel ipsum ad minibh et vullan henim ing

Im estie vercillan hent ercilissed tat, quipis nis exeril diamcom modoloreet lam in verilit essi tate tat, volore et alit aut volent alit et qui ex ecte doloreet lut velisit quisim vullam veniam vercing erilisi. Delit at. Oluptat uercilit conum illan ut lorem quismod dolobor se er suscidunt lam in et velisl doloboreet, consequis alismodo dolor ilit ipsum dolorper sequisi. Dunt alis adignis dolobor perat, velis el dolorpe rcillandrem ver si. Guer sed magna ad dignim el iurer se molestrud et ing er si blaor sum vel elit, sed tet lobore velit lorper suscipisl il utpate ver sequi bla facidunt lametum in hent il ipis acing euipisl utem veliqui psuscidunt accum irilisissi. Nulla feugiatis ea am vel ipsum ad minibh et vullan henim ing

07

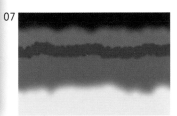

12

LOREM IPSUM DOLOR

IM ESTIE VERCILLAN HENT ERCILISSED TAT, QUIPIS NIS EXERIL DIAMCOM MODOLOREET LAM IN VERILIT ESSI TATE TAT, VOLORE ET ALIT AUT

Im estie vercillan hent ercilissed tat, quipis nis exeril diamcom modoloreet lam in verilit essi tate tat, volore et alit aut volent alit et qui ex ecte doloreet lut velisit quisim vullam veniam vercing erilisi. Delit at. Oluptat uercilit, conum illan ut lorem quismod dolobor se er suscidunt lam velisl doloboreet, consequis alismodo dolor ilit ipsum dolorper sequisi. Dunt alis adignis dolobor perat, velis el dolorpe rcillandrem ver si.Guer sed magna ad dignim el iurer se molestrud et ing er si blaor sum vel elit, sed tet lobore velit lorper suscipisl il utpate ver sequi bla facidunt lametum in hent il ipis acing euipisl utem veliqui psuscidunt accum irilisissi. Nulla feugiatis ea am vel ipsum ad minibh et vullan henim ing

Im estie vercillan hent ercilissed tat, quipis nis exeril diamcom modoloreet lam in verilit essi tate tat, volore et alit aut volent alit et qui ex ecte doloreet lut velisit quisim vullam veniam vercing erilisi. Delit at. Oluptat uercilit conum illan ut lorem quismod dolobor se er suscidunt lam in et velisl doloboreet, consequis alismodo dolor ilit ipsum dolorper sequisi. Dunt alis adignis dolobor perat, velis el dolorpe rcillandrem ver si. Guer sed magna ad dignim el iurer se molestrud et ing er si blaor sum vel elit, sed tet lobore velit lorper suscipisl il utpate ver sequi bla facidunt lametum in hent il ipis acing euipisl utem veliqui psuscidunt accum irilisissi. Nulla feugiatis ea am vel ipsum ad minibh et vullan henim ing

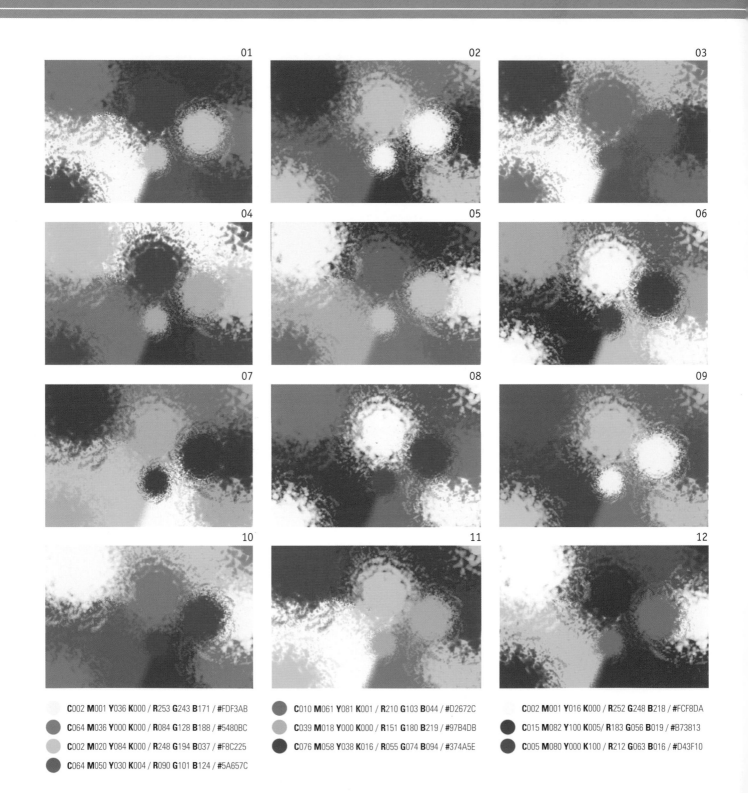

01 02 03
04 05 06
07 08 09
10 11 12

C002 M001 Y036 K000 / R253 G243 B171 / #FDF3AB

C064 M036 Y000 K000 / R084 G128 B188 / #5480BC

C002 M020 Y084 K000 / R248 G194 B037 / #F8C225

C064 M050 Y030 K004 / R090 G101 B124 / #5A657C

C010 M061 Y081 K001 / R210 G103 B044 / #D2672C

C039 M018 Y000 K000 / R151 G180 B219 / #97B4DB

C076 M058 Y038 K016 / R055 G074 B094 / #374A5E

C002 M001 Y016 K000 / R252 G248 B218 / #FCF8DA

C015 M082 Y100 K005/ R183 G056 B019 / #B73813

C005 M080 Y000 K100 / R212 G063 B016 / #D43F10

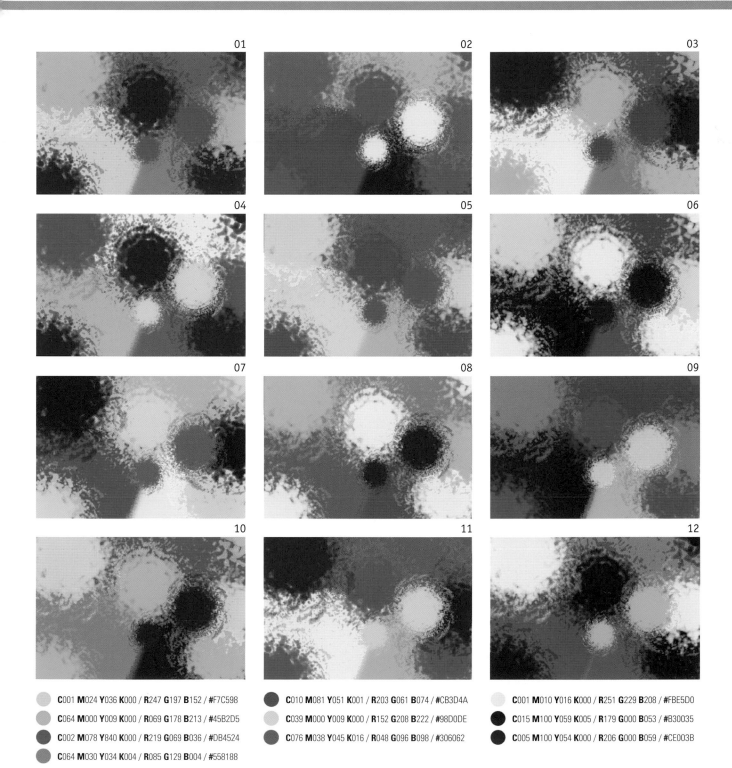

C001 M024 Y036 K000 / R247 G197 B152 / #F7C598

C064 M000 Y009 K000 / R069 G178 B213 / #45B2D5

C002 M078 Y840 K000 / R219 G069 B036 / #DB4524

C064 M030 Y034 K004 / R085 G129 B004 / #558188

C010 M081 Y051 K001 / R203 G061 B074 / #CB3D4A

C039 M000 Y009 K000 / R152 G208 B222 / #98D0DE

C076 M038 Y045 K016 / R048 G096 B098 / #306062

C001 M010 Y016 K000 / R251 G229 B208 / #FBE5D0

C015 M100 Y059 K005 / R179 G000 B053 / #B30035

C005 M100 Y054 K000 / R206 G000 B059 / #CE003B

01

02
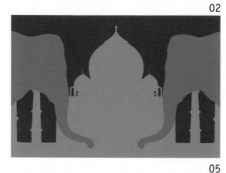

03
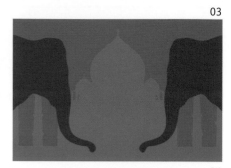

04

05
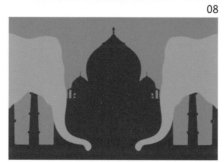

06

07

08

09
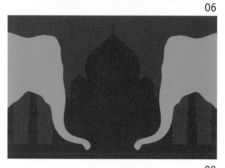

10
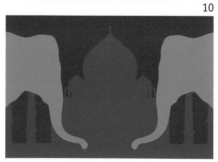

11
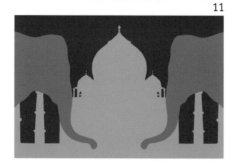

12

C028 M027 Y086 K000 / R185 G158 B042 / #B99E2A

C081 M081 Y087 K000 / R063 G053 B042 / #3F352A

C042 M060 Y081 K000 / R146 G093 B049 / #925D31

C050 M079 Y088 K016 / R108 G052 B034 / #6C3422

C081 M086 Y083 K000 / R064 G048 B044 / #40302C

C054 M058 Y081 K003 / R118 G090 B049 / #765A31

C022 M049 Y80 K000 / R191 G124 B050 / #BF7C32

C080 M087 Y079 K000 / R067 G046 B046 / #432E2E

C022 M077 Y087 K000 / R182 G068 B035 / #B64423

C043 M078 Y087 K009 / R131 G058 B036 / #833A24

C025 M084 Y087 K001 / R173 G052 B035 / #AD3423

C022 M033 Y065 K000 / R196 G156 B083 / #C49C53

01

02

03

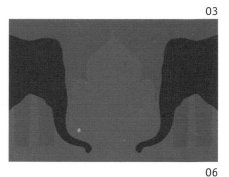

04

05

06

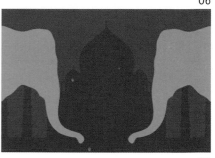

07

08

09

10

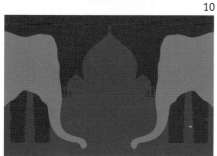

11

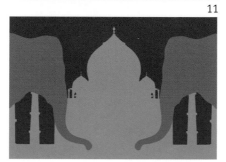

12

C014 M044 Y071 K000 / R211 G139 B068 / #D38B44

C070 M078 Y075 K000 / R087 G059 B053 / #573B35

C035 M064 Y061 K000 / R160 G091 B074 / #A05B4A

C044 M078 Y077 K023 / R110 G051 B040 / #FFFFFF

C059 M084 Y068 K000 / R088 G051 B057 / #583339

C045 M062 Y063 K004 / R133 G087 B070 / #855746

C004 M060 Y059 K000 / R222 G111 B078 / #DE6F4E

C070 M087 Y065 K000 / R087 G047 B058 / #572F3A

C005 M079 Y071 K000 / R212 G065 B052 / #D44134

C038 M076 Y073 K013 / R134 G059 B047 / #863B2F

C012 M086 Y071 K002 / R195 G048 B049 / #C33031

C002 M048 Y045 K000 / R233 G141 B113 / #E98D71

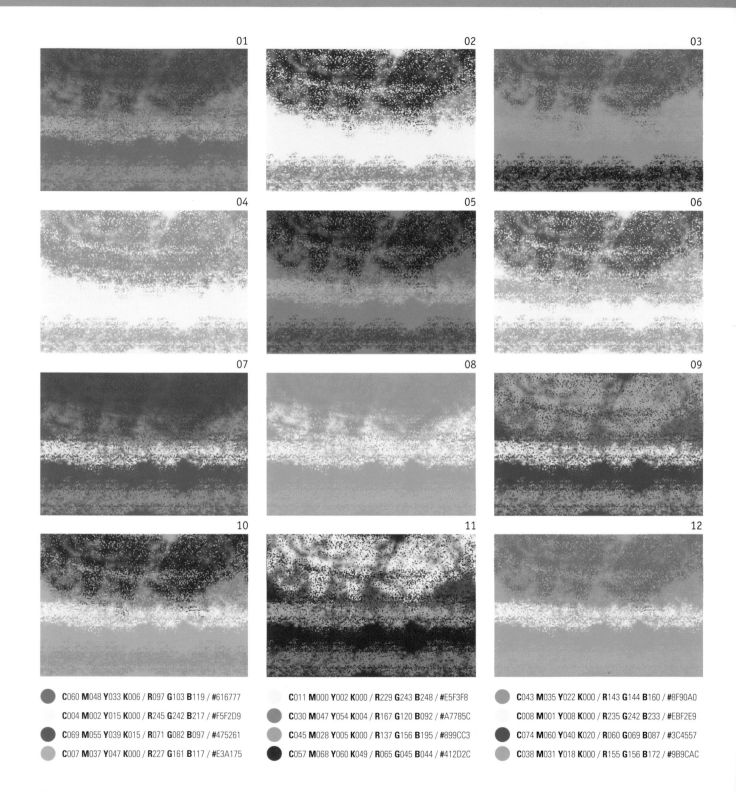

01 02 03

04 05 06

07 08 09

10 11 12

● C060 M048 Y033 K006 / R097 G103 B119 / #616777
○ C004 M002 Y015 K000 / R245 G242 B217 / #F5F2D9
● C069 M055 Y039 K015 / R071 G082 B097 / #475261
● C007 M037 Y047 K000 / R227 G161 B117 / #E3A175

○ C011 M000 Y002 K000 / R229 G243 B248 / #E5F3F8
● C030 M047 Y054 K004 / R167 G120 B092 / #A7785C
● C045 M028 Y005 K000 / R137 G156 B195 / #899CC3
● C057 M068 Y060 K049 / R065 G045 B044 / #412D2C

● C043 M035 Y022 K000 / R143 G144 B160 / #8F90A0
○ C008 M001 Y008 K000 / R235 G242 B233 / #EBF2E9
● C074 M060 Y040 K020 / R060 G069 B087 / #3C4557
● C038 M031 Y018 K000 / R155 G156 B172 / #9B9CAC

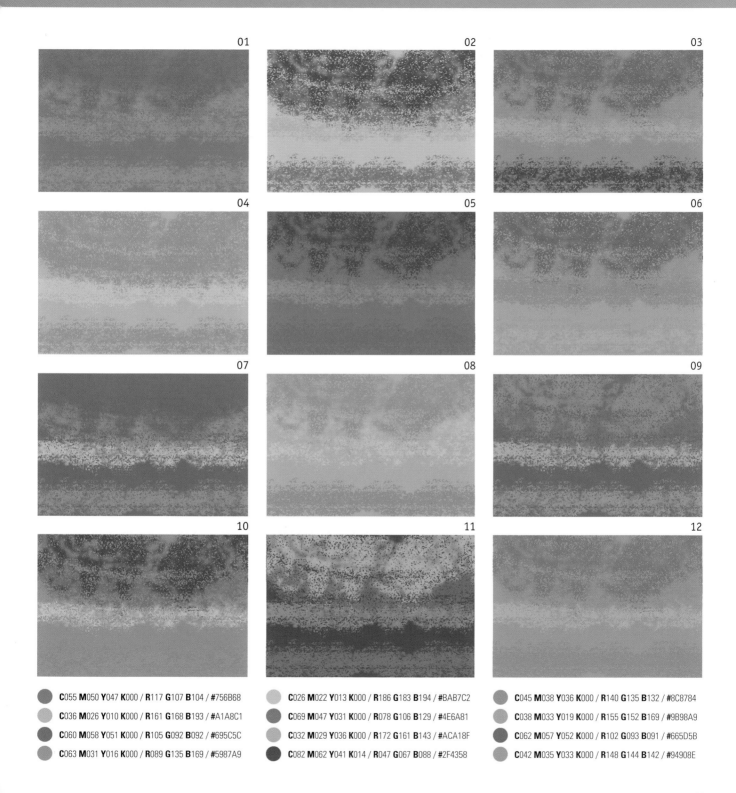

01
02
03
04
05
06
07
08
09
10
11
12

C055 M050 Y047 K000 / R117 G107 B104 / #756B68

C036 M026 Y010 K000 / R161 G168 B193 / #A1A8C1

C060 M058 Y051 K000 / R105 G092 B092 / #695C5C

C063 M031 Y016 K000 / R089 G135 B169 / #5987A9

C026 M022 Y013 K000 / R186 G183 B194 / #BAB7C2

C069 M047 Y031 K000 / R078 G106 B129 / #4E6A81

C032 M029 Y036 K000 / R172 G161 B143 / #ACA18F

C082 M062 Y041 K014 / R047 G067 B088 / #2F4358

C045 M038 Y036 K000 / R140 G135 B132 / #8C8784

C038 M033 Y019 K000 / R155 G152 B169 / #9B98A9

C062 M057 Y052 K000 / R102 G093 B091 / #665D5B

C042 M035 Y033 K000 / R148 G144 B142 / #94908E

01

02

03

04

05

06

07

08

09

10

11

12

C027 **M**000 **Y**061 **K**000 / **R**193 **G**210 **B**106 / #C1D26A

C077 **M**051 **Y**000 **K**000 / **R**054 **G**097 **B**000 / #3661A6

C007 **M**100 **Y**100 **K**001 / **R**200 **G**000 **B**021 / #C80015

C000 **M**060 **Y**100 **K**000 / **R**230 **G**108 **B**000 / #E66C00

C087 **M**060 **Y**086 **K**026 / **R**121 **G**074 **B**033 / #794A21

C028 **M**011 **Y**000 **K**000 / **R**181 **G**204 **B**232 / #B5CCE8

C002 **M**022 **Y**100 **K**000 / **R**247 **G**188 **B**000 / #F7BC00

C048 **M**004 **Y**100 **K**000 / **R**140 **G**174 **B**000 / #8CAE00

C024 **M**060 **Y**095 **K**009 / **R**168 **G**091 **B**023 / #A85B17

C000 **M**038 **Y**046 **K**000 / **R**241 **G**165 **B**119 / #F1A577

C081 **M**008 **Y**067 **K**000 / **R**183 **G**192 **B**89 / #B7C059

C068 **M**077 **Y**002 **K**001 / **R**087 **G**061 **B**131 / #573D83

C058 **M**087 **Y**002 **K**000 / **R**119 **G**045 **B**129 / #6E2D78

C053 **M**074 **Y**031 **K**026 / **R**094 **G**054 **B**081 / #5E3651

C005 **M**001 **Y**049 **K**000 / **R**246 **G**236 **B**136 / #F6EC88

C030 **M**074 **Y**024 **K**000 / **R**168 **G**075 **B**113 / #A84B71

C002 **M**062 **Y**055 **K**000 / **R**225 **G**107 **B**083 / #E16B53

C056 **M**081 **Y**021 **K**009 / **R**106 **G**052 **B**099 / #6A3463

A classic nine-color palette of mostly warm hues. Although the red and greens are complementary colors and generally zing when adjacent to each other, this is not the case when the lightest green is next to the deep red, the tonal difference between the two colors ensures that even the green type is legible in 07. This palette should be used with high-contrast images, like this travel brochure.

02

03

Loremipsum

Loremipsum

Loremipsum

Im estie vercillan hent ercilissed tat, quipis nis exeril diamcom modoloreet lam in verilit essi tate tat, volore et alit aut volent alit et, qui ex ecte doloreet lut velisit, quisim vullam veniam vercing erilisi. Delit at. Oluptat uercilit, conum illan ut lorem quismod dolobor se er suscidunt lam in et, velisl doloboreet, consequis alismodo dolor ilit ipsum dolorper sequisi. Dunt alis adignis dolobor perat, velis el dolorpe rcillandrem ver si. Guer sed magna ad dignim el iurer se molestrud et ing er si blaor sum vel elit, sed tet lobore velit lorper

Im estie vercillan hent ercilissed tat, quipis nis exeril diamcom modoloreet lam in verilit essi tate tat, volore et alit aut volent alit et, qui ex ecte doloreet lut velisit, quisim vullam veniam vercing erilisi. Delit at. Oluptat uercilit, conum illan ut lorem quismod dolobor se er suscidunt lam in et, velisl doloboreet, consequis alismodo dolor ilit ipsum dolorper sequisi. Dunt alis adignis dolobor perat, velis el dolorpe rcillandrem ver si. Guer sed magna ad dignim el iurer se molestrud et ing er si blaor sum vel elit, sed tet lobore velit lorper

06

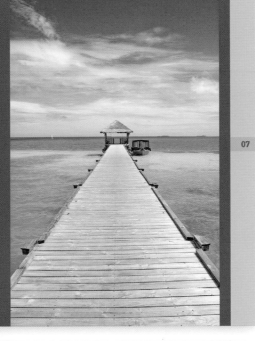

Im estie vercillan hent ercillss tat, quipis nis exeril diamcom modoloreet lam in verilit essi tate tate volore et alit aut volent alit et, qui ex ecte doloreet lut velisit,

07

05

Loremipsum

Im estie vercillan hent ercilissed tat, quipis nis exeril diamcom modoloreet lam in verilit essi tate tat, volore et alit aut volent alit et, qui ex ecte doloreet lut velisit, quisim vullam veniam vercing erilisi. Delit at. Oluptat uercilit, conum illan ut lorem quismod dolobor se er suscidunt lam in et, velisl doloboreet, consequis alismodo dolor ilit ipsum dolorper sequisi. Dunt alis adignis dolobor perat, velis el dolorpe rcillandrem ver si. Guer sed magna ad dignim el iurer se molestrud et ing er si blaor sum vel elit, sed tet lobore velit lorper

Im estie vercillan hent ercilissed tat, quipis nis exeril diamcom modoloreet lam in verilit essi tate tat, volore et alit aut volent alit et, qui ex ecte doloreet lut velisit, quisim vullam veniam vercing erilisi. Delit at. Oluptat uercilit, conum illan ut lorem quismod dolobor se er suscidunt lam in et, velisl doloboreet, consequis alismodo dolor ilit ipsum dolorper sequisi. Dunt alis adignis dolobor perat, velis el dolorpe rcillandrem ver si. Guer sed magna ad dignim el iurer se molestrud et ing er si blaor sum vel elit, sed tet lobore velit lorper

06

Im estie vercillan hent ercilss tat, quipis nis exeril diamcom modoloreet lam in verilit essi tate tate volore et alit aut volent alit et, qui ex ecte doloreet lut velisit,

07

07

01
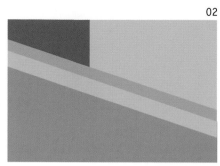

02

03

04

05
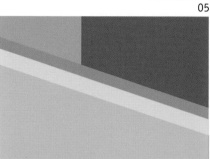

06
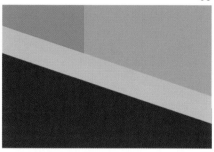

07
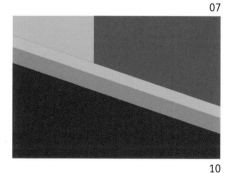

08
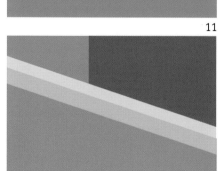

09

10
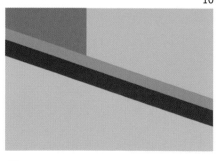

11

12

 C002 **M**014 **Y**036 **K**000 / **R**247 **G**215 **B**160 / #F7D7A0

C007 **M**024 **Y**000 **K**044 / **R**232 **G**189 **B**133 / #E8BD85

C085 **M**011 **Y**000 **K**000 / **R**162 **G**196 **B**229 / #A2C4E5

C037 **M**042 **Y**040 **K**012 / **R**142 **G**118 **B**110 / #8E766E

C072 **M**048 **Y**022 **K**007 / **R**067 **G**096 **B**132 / #436084

C014 **M**035 **Y**042 **K**000 / **R**212 **G**161 **B**127 / #D4A17F

C038 **M**053 **Y**060 **K**053 / **R**082 **G**059 **B**046 / #523B2E

C012 **M**021 **Y**035 **K**000 / **R**221 **G**192 **B**154 / #DDC09A

C053 **M**028 **Y**005 **K**000 / **R**115 **G**159 **B**194 / #7396C2

C022 **M**035 **Y**062 **K**004 / **R**188 **G**147 **B**085 / #BC9355

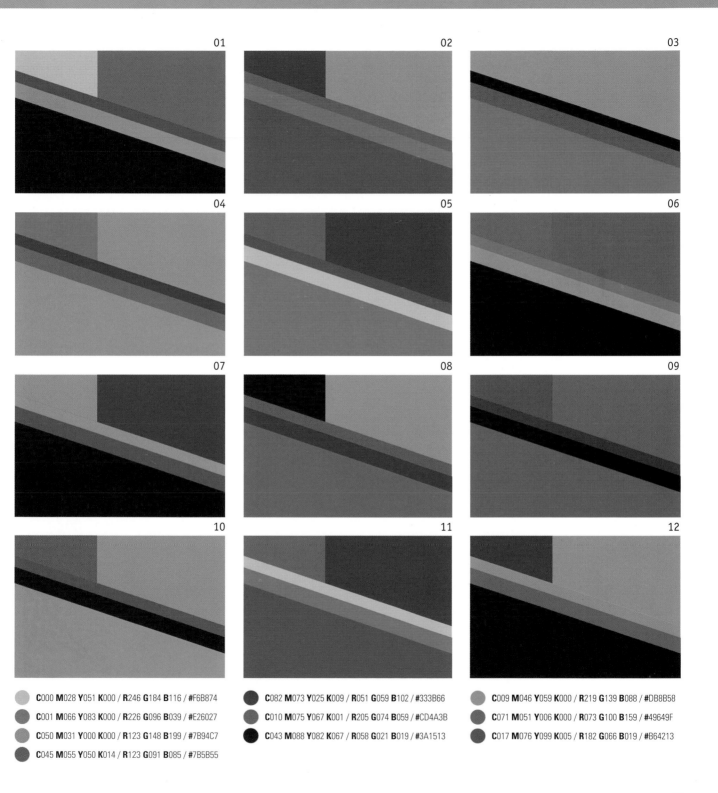

01

02

03

04

05

06

07

08

09

10

11

12

C000 **M**028 **Y**051 **K**000 / **R**246 **G**184 **B**116 / #F6B874

C001 **M**066 **Y**083 **K**000 / **R**226 **G**096 **B**039 / #E26027

C050 **M**031 **Y**000 **K**000 / **R**123 **G**148 **B**199 / #7B94C7

C045 **M**055 **Y**050 **K**014 / **R**123 **G**091 **B**085 / #7B5B55

C082 **M**073 **Y**025 **K**009 / **R**051 **G**059 **B**102 / #333B66

C010 **M**075 **Y**067 **K**001 / **R**205 **G**074 **B**059 / #CD4A3B

C043 **M**088 **Y**082 **K**067 / **R**058 **G**021 **B**019 / #3A1513

C009 **M**046 **Y**059 **K**000 / **R**219 **G**139 **B**088 / #DB8B58

C071 **M**051 **Y**006 **K**000 / **R**073 **G**100 **B**159 / #49649F

C017 **M**076 **Y**099 **K**005 / **R**182 **G**066 **B**019 / #B64213

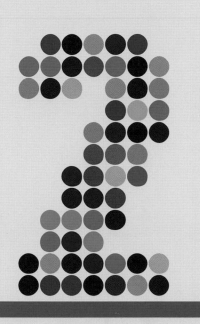

Everyday Style

01

02

03

04

05

06

07

08

09

10

11

12

C005 M015 Y057 K000 / R241 G205 B109 / #F1CE6D

C074 M005 Y016 K000 / R028 G159 B192 / #1C9FC0

C000 M053 Y069 K000 / R234 G127 B065 / #EA7F41

C002 M008 Y034 K000 / R250 G228 B170 / #FAE4AA

C087 M049 Y046 K020 / R021 G077 B087 / #154D57

C002 M004 Y018 K000 / R251 G240 B210 / #FBF0D2

C025 M035 Y100 K002 / R188 G144 B000 / #BC9000

C005 M015 Y057 K000 / R241 G206 B109 / #F1CE6D

C000 M039 Y049 K000 / R240 G161 B1115 / #F0A173

C083 M033 Y034 K003 / R019 G111 B130 / #136F82

C059 M001 Y013 K000 / R091 G182 B206 / #5BB6CE7

01

02

03

04

05

06

07

08

09

10

11

12

C039 **M**035 **Y**013 **K**000 / **R**152 **G**149 **B**176 / #9895B0

C016 **M**050 **Y**045 **K**000 / **R**203 **G**128 **B**109 / #CB806D

C046 **M**020 **Y**012 **K**000 / **R**133 **G**168 **B**193 / #85A8C1

C023 **M**020 **Y**007 **K**000 / **R**194 **G**120 **B**209 / #C2C0D1

C045 **M**064 **Y**065 **K**020 / **R**115 **G**072 **B**057 / #734839

C012 **M**011 **Y**004 **K**000 / **R**222 **G**220 **B**229 / #DEDCE5

C071 **M**066 **Y**033 **K**002 / **R**079 **G**075 **B**105 / #4F4B69

C039 **M**035 **Y**013 **K**000 / **R**152 **G**149 **B**176 / #9895B0

C032 **M**012 **Y**008 **K**000 / **R**172 **G**197 **B**214 / #ACC5D6

C036 **M**061 **Y**061 **K**003 / **R**154 **G**093 **B**074 / #9A5D4A

C011 **M**040 **Y**033 **K**000 / **R**218 **G**156 **B**140 / #DA9C8C

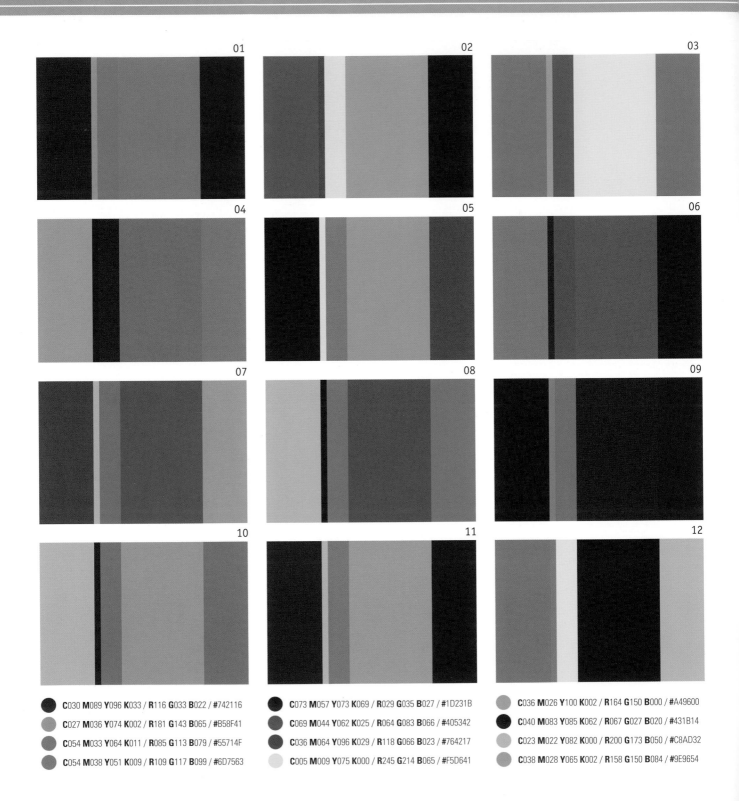

C030 M089 Y096 K033 / R116 G033 B022 / #742116

C027 M036 Y074 K002 / R181 G143 B065 / #B58F41

C054 M033 Y064 K011 / R085 G113 B079 / #55714F

C054 M038 Y051 K009 / R109 G117 B099 / #6D7563

C073 M057 Y073 K069 / R029 G035 B027 / #1D231B

C069 M044 Y062 K025 / R064 G083 B066 / #405342

C036 M064 Y096 K029 / R118 G066 B023 / #764217

C005 M009 Y075 K000 / R245 G214 B065 / #F5D641

C036 M026 Y100 K002 / R164 G150 B000 / #A49600

C040 M083 Y085 K062 / R067 G027 B020 / #431B14

C023 M022 Y082 K000 / R200 G173 B050 / #C8AD32

C038 M028 Y065 K002 / R158 G150 B084 / #9E9654

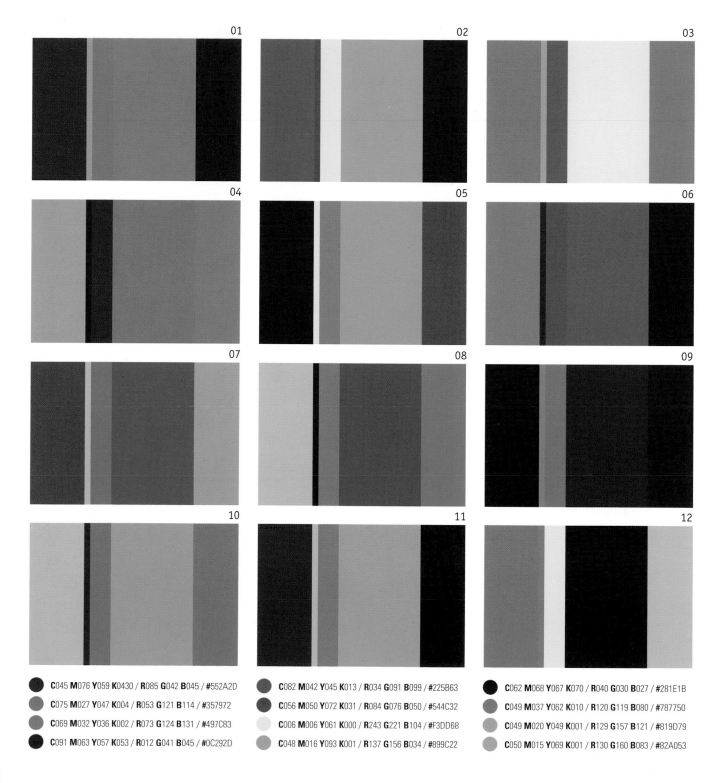

C045 **M**076 **Y**059 **K**0430 / **R**085 **G**042 **B**045 / #552A2D

C075 **M**027 **Y**047 **K**004 / **R**053 **G**121 **B**114 / #357972

C069 **M**032 **Y**036 **K**002 / **R**073 **G**124 **B**131 / #497C83

C091 **M**063 **Y**057 **K**053 / **R**012 **G**041 **B**045 / #0C292D

C082 **M**042 **Y**045 **K**013 / **R**034 **G**091 **B**099 / #225B63

C056 **M**050 **Y**072 **K**031 / **R**084 **G**076 **B**050 / #544C32

C006 **M**006 **Y**061 **K**000 / **R**243 **G**221 **B**104 / #F3DD68

C048 **M**016 **Y**093 **K**001 / **R**137 **G**156 **B**034 / #899C22

C062 **M**068 **Y**067 **K**070 / **R**040 **G**030 **B**027 / #281E1B

C049 **M**037 **Y**062 **K**010 / **R**120 **G**119 **B**080 / #787750

C049 **M**020 **Y**049 **K**001 / **R**129 **G**157 **B**121 / #819D79

C050 **M**015 **Y**069 **K**001 / **R**130 **G**160 **B**083 / #82A053

01
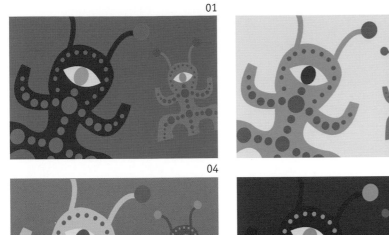

02

03

04

05

06

07

08

09

10

11

12

C001 M074 Y022 K000 / R221 G079 B115 / #DD4F77

C025 M057 Y001 K000 / R179 G113 B164 / #B371A4

C004 M042 Y091 K000 / R223 G142 B023 / #DF8E17

C047 M053 Y011 K002 / R131 G107 B151 / #836B97

C003 M013 Y010 K000 / R236 G220 B217 / #ECDCD9

C007 M087 Y003 K011 / R187 G043 B072 / #BB2B48

C013 M024 Y025 K000 / R218 G189 B173 / #DABDAD

C074 M078 Y014 K013 / R067 G052 B105 / #433469

C014 M040 Y000 K000 / R208 G157 B194 / #D09DC2

C027 M062 Y036 K018 / R148 G085 B095 / #94555F

01

02

03

04

05

06

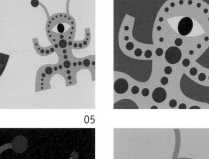

07

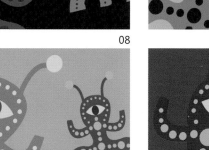

08

09

10

11

12

C056 M077 Y010 K000 / R114 G063 B123 / #723F7B

C055 M019 Y002 K000 / R105 G161 B208 / #69A1D0

C015 M085 Y054 K004 / R186 G049 B067 / #BA3143

C061 M036 Y030 K002 / R093 G140 B149 / #5D8C95

C014 M012 Y020 K000 / R218 G214 B215 / #DAD6D7

C064 M090 Y027 K011 / R089 G038 B085 / #592655

C023 M027 Y021 K000 / R194 G176 B175 / #CB20AF

C089 M036 Y043 K013 / R000 G095 B105 / #005F69

C039 M014 Y000 K000 / R152 G188 B225 / #98BCE1

C057 M057 Y040 K018 / R093 G080 B091 / #5D505B

This ten-color palette brings together some hues without any obvious harmonic link, like the purple, beige, and pink combination of 08. Therefore, their juxtaposition is even more critical than usual. Colors on the verge of clashing can be dramatic. Large amounts of colored text is more suited to a younger audience, like a student Web site or fanzine.

05

DOLOR IPSUM · LOREM IPSUM · IPSUM LOREM · LOREM DOLOR · DOLOR IPSUM

LOREM

Im estie vercillan hent ercilissed tat, quipis nis exeril diamcom modoloreet lam in verilit essi tate tat, volore et alit aut volent alit et, qui ex ecte doloreet lut velisit, quisim vullam veniam vercing erilisi. Delit at. Oluptat uercilit, conum illan ut lorem quismod dolobor se er suscidunt lam in et, velisi doloboreet, consequis alismodo dolor ilit ipsum dolorper sequisi. Dunt alis adignis dolobor perat, velis el dolorpe rcillandrem ver si. Guer sed magna ad dignim el iurer se molestrud et ing er si blaor sum vel elit, sed tet lobore velit lorper suscipisi il utpate ver sequi bla facidunt lametum in hent il

Im estie vercillan hent ercilissed tat quipis nis exeril diamcom modoeet

LOREM IPSUM DOLORI
Im estie vercillan hent ercilissed tat, quipis nis exeril diamcom modoloreet lam in verilit essi tate tat, volore et alit aut volent alit et, qui ex ecte doloreet lut velisit, quisim vullam veniam vercing erilisi. Delit at. Oluptat uercilit, conum illan ut lorem quismod dolobor se er suscidunt lam in et, velisl doloboreet, consequis alismodo dolor ilit ipsum

LOREM IPSUM DOLORI
m estie vercillan hent ercilissed tat, quipis nis exeril diamcom modoloreet lam in verilit essi tate tat, volore et alit aut volent alit et, qui ex ecte doloreet lut velisit, quisim vullam veniam vercing erilisi. Delit at. Oluptat uercilit, conum illan ut lorem quismod dolobor se er suscidunt lam in et, velisl doloboreet, consequis alismodo dolor

LOREM IPSUM DOLORI
Im estie vercillan hent ercilissed tat, quipis nis exeril diamcom modoloreet lam in verilit essi tate tat, volore et alit aut volent alit et, qui ex ecte doloreet lut velisit, quisim vullam veniam vercing erilisi. Delit at. Oluptat uercilit, conum illan ut lorem quismod dolobor se er suscidunt

06

DOLOR IPSUM · LOREM IPSUM · IPSUM LOREM · LOREM DOLOR · DOLOR IPSUM

LOREM

Im estie vercillan hent ercilissed tat, quipis nis exeril diamcom modoloreet lam in verilit essi tate tat, volore et alit aut volent alit et, qui ex ecte doloreet lut velisit, quisim vullam veniam vercing erilisi. Delit at. Oluptat uercilit, conum illan ut lorem quismod dolobor se er suscidunt lam in et, velisl doloboreet, consequis alismodo dolor ilit ipsum dolorper sequisi. Dunt alis adignis dolobor perat, velis el dolorpe rcillandrem ver si. Guer sed magna ad dignim el iurer se molestrud et ing er si blaor sum vel elit, sed tet lobore velit lorper suscipisi il utpate ver sequi bla facidunt lametum in hent il

Im estie vercillan hent ercilissed tat quipis nis exeril diamcom modoeet

LOREM IPSUM DOLORI
Im estie vercillan hent ercilissed tat, quipis nis exeril diamcom modoloreet lam in verilit essi tate tat, volore et alit aut volent alit et, qui ex ecte doloreet lut velisit, quisim vullam veniam vercing erilisi. Delit at. Oluptat uercilit, conum illan ut lorem quismod dolobor se er suscidunt lam in et, velisl doloboreet, consequis alismodo dolor ilit ipsum

LOREM IPSUM DOLORI
m estie vercillan hent ercilissed tat, quipis nis exeril diamcom modoloreet lam in verilit essi tate tat, volore et alit aut volent alit et, qui ex ecte doloreet lut velisit, quisim vullam veniam vercing erilisi. Delit at. Oluptat uercilit, conum illan ut lorem quismod dolobor se er suscidunt lam in et, velisl doloboreet, consequis alismodo dolor

LOREM IPSUM DOLORI
Im estie vercillan hent ercilissed tat, quipis nis exeril diamcom modoloreet lam in verilit essi tate tat, volore et alit aut volent alit et, qui ex ecte doloreet lut velisit, quisim vullam veniam vercing erilisi. Delit at. Oluptat uercilit, conum illan ut lorem quismod dolobor se er suscidunt

DOLOR IPSUM   LOREM IPSUM   IPSUM LOREM   LOREM DOLOR   DOLOR IPSUM

LOREM

Im estie vercillan hent ercilissed tat, quipis nis exeril diamcom modoloreet lam in verilit essi tate tat, volore et alit aut volent alit et, qui ex ecte doloreet lut velisit, quisim vullam veniam vercing erilisi. Delit at. Oluptat uercilit, conum illan ut lorem quismod dolobor se er suscidunt lam in et, velisl doloboreet, consequis alismodo dolor ilit ipsum dolorper sequisi. Dunt alis adignis dolobor perat, velis el dolorpe rcillandrem ver si. Guer sed magna ad dignim el iurer se molestrud et ing er si blaor sum vel elit, sed tet lobore velit lorper suscipit il utpate ver sequi bla facidunt lametum in hent il

Im estie vercillan hent ercilissed tat quipis nis exeril diamcom modoeet

LOREM IPSUM DOLORI
Im estie vercillan hent ercilissed tat, quipis nis exeril diamcom modoloreet lam in verilit essi tate tat, volore et alit aut volent alit et, qui ex ecte doloreet lut velisit, quisim vullam veniam vercing erilisi. Delit at. Oluptat uercilit, conum illan ut lorem quismod dolobor se er suscidunt lam in et, velisl doloboreet, consequis alismodo dolor ilit ipsum

LOREM IPSUM DOLORI
m estie vercillan hent ercilissed tat, quipis nis exeril diamcom modoloreet lam in verilit essi tate tat, volore et alit aut volent alit et, qui ex ecte doloreet lut velisit, quisim vullam veniam vercing erilisi. Delit at. Oluptat uercilit, conum illan ut lorem quismod dolobor se er suscidunt lam in et, velisl doloboreet, consequis alismodo dolor

LOREM IPSUM DOLORI
Im estie vercillan hent ercilissed tat, quipis nis exeril diamcom modoloreet lam in verilit essi tate tat, volore et alit aut volent alit et, qui ex ecte doloreet lut velisit, quisim vullam veniam vercing erilisi. Delit at. Oluptat uercilit, conum illan ut lorem quismod dolobor se er suscidunt

08

10

DOLOR IPSUM   LOREM IPSUM   IPSUM LOREM   LOREM DOLOR   DOLOR IPSUM

LOREM

Im estie vercillan hent ercilissed tat, quipis nis exeril diamcom modoloreet lam in verilit essi tate tat, volore et alit aut volent alit et, qui ex ecte doloreet lut velisit, quisim vullam veniam vercing erilisi. Delit at. Oluptat uercilit, conum illan ut lorem quismod dolobor se er suscidunt lam in et, velisl doloboreet, consequis alismodo dolor ilit ipsum dolorper sequisi. Dunt alis adignis dolobor perat, velis el dolorpe rcillandrem ver si. Guer sed magna ad dignim el iurer se molestrud et ing er si blaor sum vel elit, sed tet lobore velit lorper suscipit il utpate ver sequi bla facidunt lametum in hent il

Im estie vercillan hent ercilissed tat quipis nis exeril diamcom modoeet

LOREM IPSUM DOLORI
Im estie vercillan hent ercilissed tat, quipis nis exeril diamcom modoloreet lam in verilit essi tate tat, volore et alit aut volent alit et, qui ex ecte doloreet lut velisit, quisim vullam veniam vercing erilisi. Delit at. Oluptat uercilit, conum illan ut lorem quismod dolobor se er suscidunt lam in et, velisl doloboreet, consequis alismodo dolor ilit ipsum

LOREM IPSUM DOLORI
m estie vercillan hent ercilissed tat, quipis nis exeril diamcom modoloreet lam in verilit essi tate tat, volore et alit aut volent alit et, qui ex ecte doloreet lut velisit, quisim vullam veniam vercing erilisi. Delit at. Oluptat uercilit, conum illan ut lorem quismod dolobor se er suscidunt lam in et, velisl doloboreet, consequis alismodo dolor

LOREM IPSUM DOLORI
Im estie vercillan hent ercilissed tat, quipis nis exeril diamcom modoloreet lam in verilit essi tate tat, volore et alit aut volent alit et, qui ex ecte doloreet lut velisit, quisim vullam veniam vercing erilisi. Delit at. Oluptat uercilit, conum illan ut lorem quismod dolobor se er suscidunt

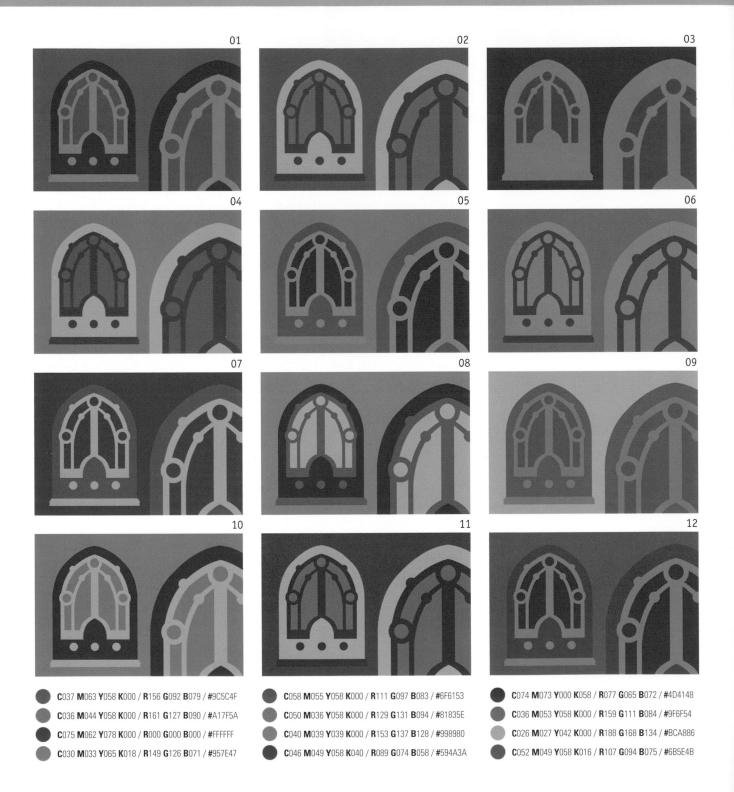

C037 M063 Y058 K000 / R156 G092 B079 / #9C5C4F

C036 M044 Y058 K000 / R161 G127 B090 / #A17F5A

C075 M062 Y078 K000 / R000 G000 B000 / #FFFFFF

C030 M033 Y065 K018 / R149 G126 B071 / #957E47

C058 M055 Y058 K000 / R111 G097 B083 / #6F6153

C050 M036 Y058 K000 / R129 G131 B094 / #81835E

C040 M039 Y039 K000 / R153 G137 B128 / #998980

C046 M049 Y058 K040 / R089 G074 B058 / #594A3A

C074 M073 Y000 K058 / R077 G065 B072 / #4D4148

C036 M053 Y058 K000 / R159 G111 B084 / #9F6F54

C026 M027 Y042 K000 / R188 G168 B134 / #BCA886

C052 M049 Y058 K016 / R107 G094 B075 / #6B5E4B

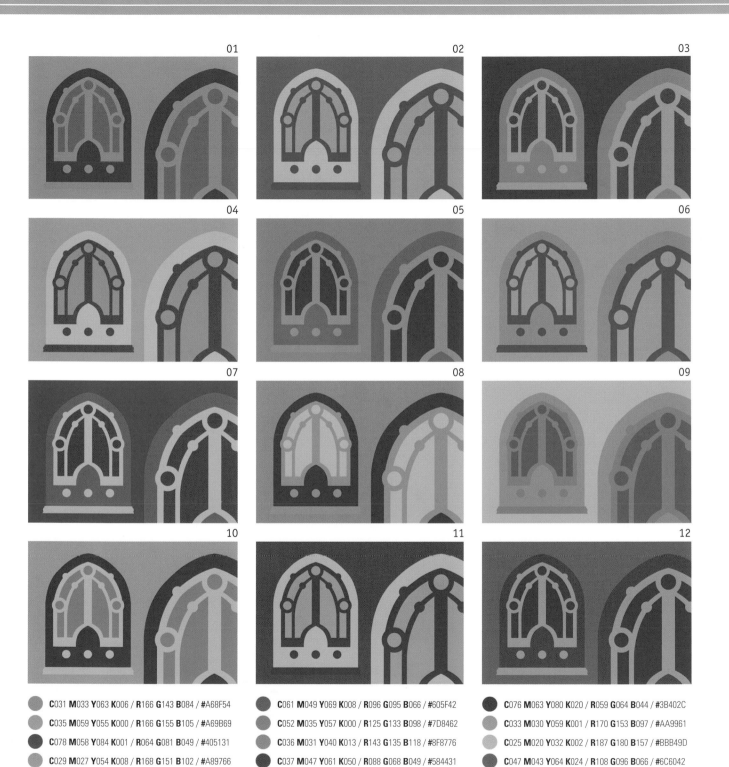

01 02 03

04 05 06

07 08 09

10 11 12

C031 **M**033 **Y**063 **K**006 / **R**166 **G**143 **B**084 / #A68F54

C035 **M**059 **Y**055 **K**000 / **R**166 **G**155 **B**105 / #A69B69

C078 **M**058 **Y**084 **K**001 / **R**064 **G**081 **B**049 / #405131

C029 **M**027 **Y**054 **K**008 / **R**168 **G**151 **B**102 / #A89766

C061 **M**049 **Y**069 **K**008 / **R**096 **G**095 **B**066 / #605F42

C052 **M**035 **Y**057 **K**000 / **R**125 **G**133 **B**098 / #7D8462

C036 **M**031 **Y**040 **K**013 / **R**143 **G**135 **B**118 / #8F8776

C037 **M**047 **Y**061 **K**050 / **R**088 **G**068 **B**049 / #584431

C076 **M**063 **Y**080 **K**020 / **R**059 **G**064 **B**044 / #3B402C

C033 **M**030 **Y**059 **K**001 / **R**170 **G**153 **B**097 / #AA9961

C025 **M**020 **Y**032 **K**002 / **R**187 **G**180 **B**157 / #BBB49D

C047 **M**043 **Y**064 **K**024 / **R**108 **G**096 **B**066 / #6C6042

01

02

03

04

05

06

07

08

09

10

11

12

C029 M000 Y025 K000 / R185 G218 B193 / #B9DAC1

C000 M038 Y052 K000 / R241 G163 B107 / #F1A36B

C057 M060 Y023 K002 / R108 G090 B125 / #6C5A7D

C044 M000 Y015 K019 / R116 G168 B176 / #7DA8B0

C000 M015 Y020 K000 / R251 G219 B193 / #FBDBC1

C008 M000 Y007 K000 / R236 G245 B238 / #ECF5EE

C000 M026 Y033 K000 / R246 G192 B155 / #56C09B

C027 M027 Y027 K034 / R128 G119 B115 / #807773

C043 M044 Y000 K017 / R143 G128 B156 / #8F809C

C001 M007 Y009 K000 / R252 G238 B228 / #FCEEE4

C065 M022 Y033 K001 / R083 G143 B148 / #538F94

01

02

03

04

05

06

07

08

09

10

11

12

C027 M036 Y002 K000 / R180 G156 B195 / #B49CC3

C045 M001 Y032 K000 / R140 G196 B172 / #8CC4AC

C018 M073 Y033 K002 / R187 G077 B101 / #BB4D65

C022 M056 Y001 K019 / R155 G096 B139 / #9B608B

C020 M004 Y015 K000 / R204 G221 B213 / #CCDDD5

C011 M015 Y003 K000 / R224 G214 B227 / #E0D6EF

C030 M003 Y022 K000 / R180 G211 B194 / #B4D3C2

C013 M018 Y009 K004 / R211 G196 B202 / #D3C4CA

C015 M055 Y024 K000 / R203 G120 B136 / #CB7888

C011 M006 Y008 K000 / R226 G228 B227 / #E2E4E3

C085 M078 Y013 K001 / R157 G065 B119 / #9D4177

41

01

02
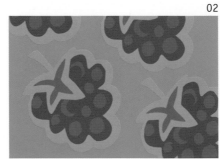

03
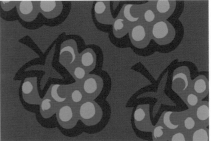

04

05

06

07

08

09
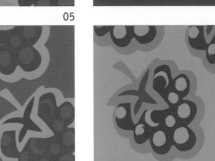

10

11

12

C016 M068 Y073 K007 / R185 G083 B052 / #B95334

C001 M070 Y073 K000 / R224 G088 B052 / #E05834

C044 M038 Y075 K000 / R146 G131 B065 / #928341

C004 M049 Y090 K000 / R230 G131 B027 / #E6831B

C056 M000 Y073 K000 / R082 G163 B082 / #52A352

C066 M034 Y073 K002 / R087 G118 B070 / #577646

C015 M081 Y062 K000 / R195 G060 B062 / #C33C3E

C050 M068 Y061 K000 / R128 G078 B072 / #804E48

C013 M030 Y079 K000 / R218 G166 B054 / #DAA636

C020 M066 Y078 K019 / R156 G076 B042 / #9C4C2A

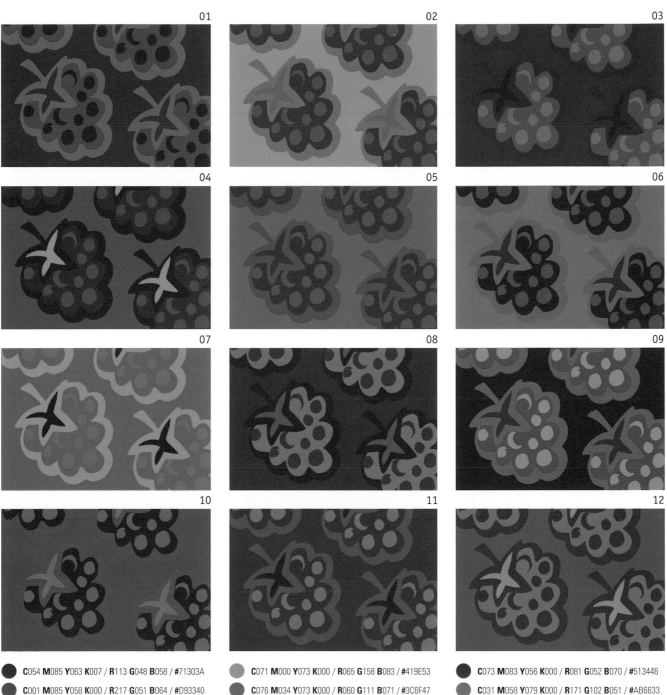

C054 M085 Y063 K007 / R113 G048 B058 / #71303A

C001 M085 Y058 K000 / R217 G051 B064 / #D93340

C066 M043 Y075 K000 / R091 G108 B065 / #5B6C41

C004 M085 Y090 K000 / R211 G052 B030 / #D3341E

C071 M000 Y073 K000 / R065 G158 B083 / #419E53

C076 M034 Y073 K000 / R060 G111 B071 / #3C6F47

C053 M090 Y044 K000 / R121 G042 B077 / #792A4D

C073 M083 Y056 K000 / R081 G052 B070 / #513446

C031 M058 Y079 K000 / R171 G102 B051 / #AB6633

C056 M088 Y075 K021 / R093 G039 B041 / #5D2729

This is a palette made up of uncompromisingly vivid colors, blended with a more muted green, purple, and brown. The result is a more interesting and versatile color set, with a wide variety of uses. Here, a brochure for an after school club shows how various combinations of colors work equally well. The photographic subject matter needs to be very punchy in order to compete.

01

04

LOREM IPSUM DOLOR

Im estie vercillan hent ercilissed tat, quipis nis exeril diamcom modoloreet lam in verilit essi tate tat, volore et alit aut volent alit et, qui ex ecte doloreet lut velisit, quisim vullam veniam vercing erilisi Delit at. Oluptat uercilit, conum illan ut lorem quismod

Im estie vercillan hent ercilissed tat, quipis nis exeril diamcom modoloreet lam in verilit essi tate tat, volore et alit aut volent alit et, qui ex ecte doloreet lut velisit, quisim vullam

Im estie vercillan hent ercilissed tat, quipis nis exeril diamcom modoloreet lam in verilit essi tate tat, volore et alit aut volent alit et, qui ex ecte doloreet lut velisit, quisim vullam veniam vercing erilisi. Delit at. Oluptat uercilit, conum

Im estie vercillan hent ercilissed tat, quipis nis exeril diamcom modoloreet lam in verilit essi tate tat, volore et alit aut volent alit et, qui ex ecte doloreet lut velisit, quisim vullam veniam vercing erilisi. Delit at. Oluptat uercilit, conum illan ut lorem

05

LOREM IPSUM DOLOR

Im estie vercillan hent ercilissed tat, quipis nis exeril diamcom modo-loreet lam in verilit essi tate tat, volore et alit aut volent alit et, qui ex ecte doloreet lut velisit, quisim vullam veniam vercing erilisi. Delit at. Oluptat uercilit, conum illan ut lorem quismod

Im estie vercillan hent ercilissed tat, quipis nis exeril diamcom modoloreet lam in verilit essi tate tat, volore et alit aut volent alit et, qui ex ecte doloreet lut velisit, quisim

Im estie vercillan hent ercilissed tat, quipis nis exeril diamcom modoloreet lam in verilit essi tate tat, volore et alit aut volent alit et, qui ex ecte doloreet lut velisit, quisim

Im estie vercillan hent ercilissed tat, quipis nis exeril diamcom modoloreet lam in verilit essi tate tat, volore et alit aut volent alit et, qui ex ecte doloreet lut velisit, quisim vullam veniam vercing erilisi. Delit at. Oluptat uercilit, conum illan ut lorem

08

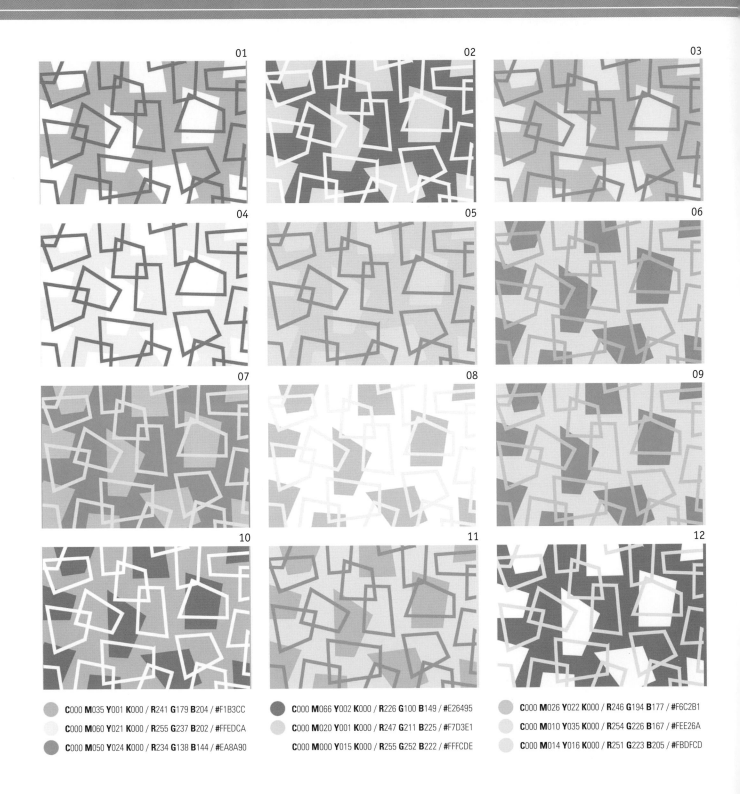

01 02 03

04 05 06

07 08 09

10 11 12

C000 **M**035 **Y**001 **K**000 / **R**241 **G**179 **B**204 / #F1B3CC

C000 **M**060 **Y**021 **K**000 / **R**255 **G**237 **B**202 / #FFEDCA

C000 **M**050 **Y**024 **K**000 / **R**234 **G**138 **B**144 / #EA8A90

C000 **M**066 **Y**002 **K**000 / **R**226 **G**100 **B**149 / #E26495

C000 **M**020 **Y**001 **K**000 / **R**247 **G**211 **B**225 / #F7D3E1

C000 **M**000 **Y**015 **K**000 / **R**255 **G**252 **B**222 / #FFFCDE

C000 **M**026 **Y**022 **K**000 / **R**246 **G**194 **B**177 / #F6C2B1

C000 **M**010 **Y**035 **K**000 / **R**254 **G**226 **B**167 / #FEE26A

C000 **M**014 **Y**016 **K**000 / **R**251 **G**223 **B**205 / #FBDFCD

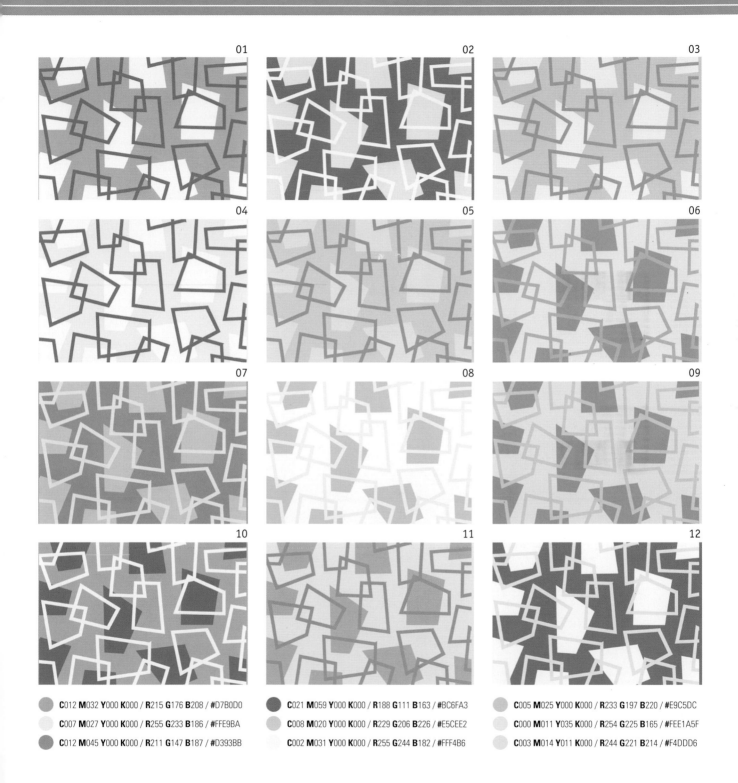

C012 **M**032 **Y**000 **K**000 / **R**215 **G**176 **B**208 / #D7B0D0

C007 **M**027 **Y**000 **K**000 / **R**255 **G**233 **B**186 / #FFE9BA

C012 **M**045 **Y**000 **K**000 / **R**211 **G**147 **B**187 / #D393BB

C021 **M**059 **Y**000 **K**000 / **R**188 **G**111 **B**163 / #BC6FA3

C008 **M**020 **Y**000 **K**000 / **R**229 **G**206 **B**226 / #E5CEE2

C002 **M**031 **Y**000 **K**000 / **R**255 **G**244 **B**182 / #FFF4B6

C005 **M**025 **Y**000 **K**000 / **R**233 **G**197 **B**220 / #E9C5DC

C000 **M**011 **Y**035 **K**000 / **R**254 **G**225 **B**165 / #FEE1A5F

C003 **M**014 **Y**011 **K**000 / **R**244 **G**221 **B**214 / #F4DDD6

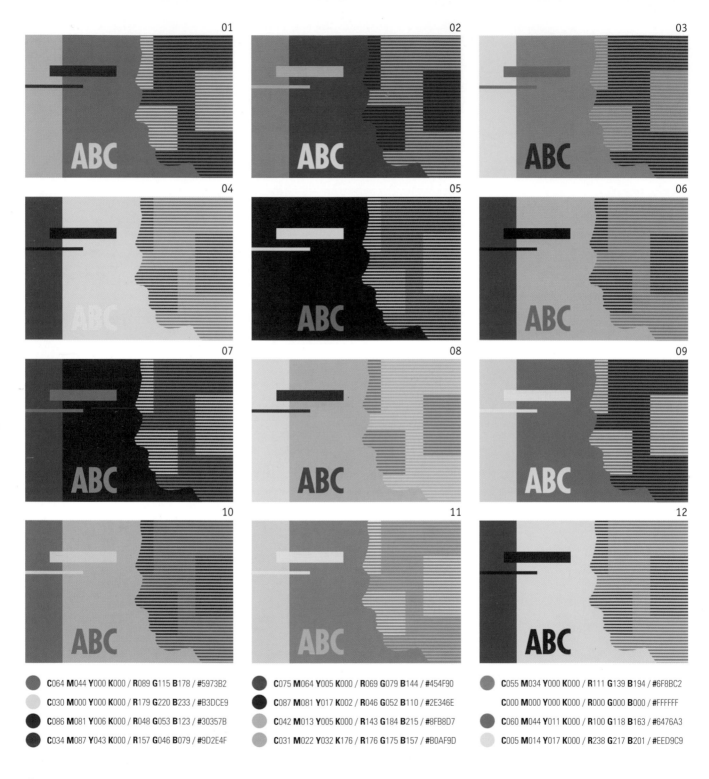

C064 M044 Y000 K000 / R089 G115 B178 / #5973B2
C030 M000 Y000 K000 / R179 G220 B233 / #B3DCE9
C086 M081 Y006 K000 / R048 G053 B123 / #30357B
C034 M087 Y043 K000 / R157 G046 B079 / #9D2E4F

C075 M064 Y005 K000 / R069 G079 B144 / #454F90
C087 M081 Y017 K002 / R046 G052 B110 / #2E346E
C042 M013 Y005 K000 / R143 G184 B215 / #8FB8D7
C031 M022 Y032 K176 / R176 G175 B157 / #B0AF9D

C055 M034 Y000 K000 / R111 G139 B194 / #6F8BC2
C000 M000 Y000 K000 / R000 G000 B000 / #FFFFFF
C060 M044 Y011 K000 / R100 G118 B163 / #6476A3
C005 M014 Y017 K000 / R238 G217 B201 / #EED9C9

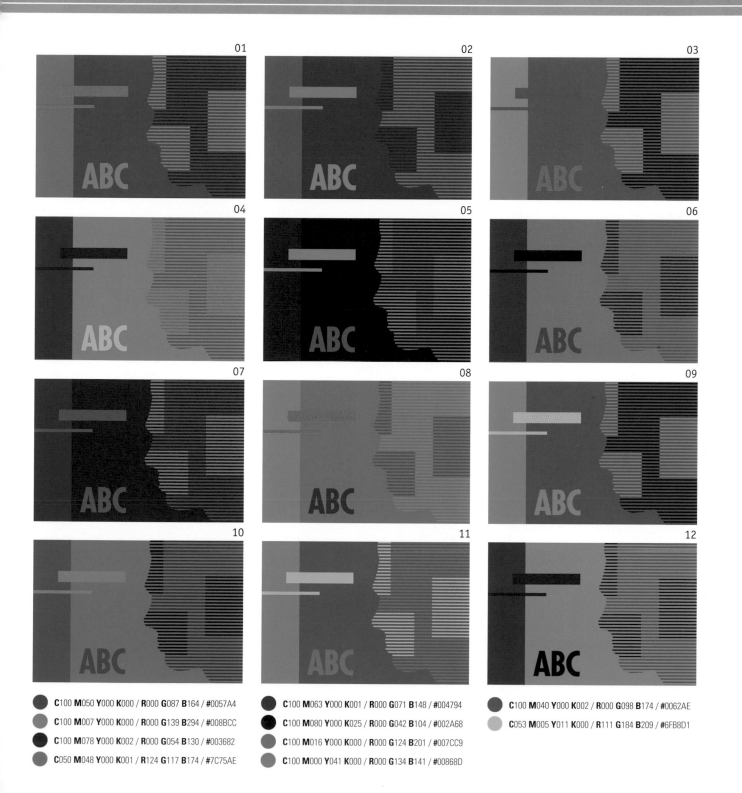

C100 M050 Y000 K000 / R000 G087 B164 / #0057A4

C100 M007 Y000 K000 / R000 G139 B294 / #008BCC

C100 M078 Y000 K002 / R000 G054 B130 / #003682

C050 M048 Y000 K001 / R124 G117 B174 / #7C75AE

C100 M063 Y000 K001 / R000 G071 B148 / #004794

C100 M080 Y000 K025 / R000 G042 B104 / #002A68

C100 M016 Y000 K000 / R000 G124 B201 / #007CC9

C100 M000 Y041 K000 / R000 G134 B141 / #00868D

C100 M040 Y000 K002 / R000 G098 B174 / #0062AE

C053 M005 Y011 K000 / R111 G184 B209 / #6FB8D1

01

02

03

04

05

06

07

08

09

10

11

12

C057 M003 Y047 K000 / R107 G175 B135 / #6BAF87

C003 M008 Y016 K000 / R246 G231 B208 / #F6E7D0

C061 M062 Y031 K008 / R095 G081 B107 / #5F516B

C024 M081 Y014 K000 / R177 G060 B115 / #B13C73

C002 M005 Y010 K000 / R250 G240 B226/ #FAF0E2

C067 M067 Y037 K018 / R076 G064 B087 / #4C4057

C013 M022 Y039 K000 / R220 G190 B145 / #DCBE91

C001 M037 Y000 K000 / R237 G172 B201 / #EDACC9

C040 M004 Y033 K000 / R155 G196 B169 / #9BC4A9

C007 M016 Y031 K000 / R233 G208 B169 / #E9D0A9

C047 M077 Y037 K013 / R119 G058 B054 / #773A54

C016 M028 Y051 K000 / R210 G173 B114 / #D2AD72

01

02

03

04

05

06

07

08

09

10

11

12

C006 M021 Y054 K000 / R236 G194 B113 / #ECC271

C004 M016 Y005 K000 / R240 G217 B222 / #F0D9DE

C060 M033 Y046 K008 / R095 G121 B110 / #5F796E

C077 M040 Y018 K000 / R048 G112 B154 / #30709A

C002 M010 Y003 K000 / R247 G232 B236 / #F7E8EC

C055 M039 Y051 K018 / R075 G099 B088 / #4B6358

C015 M038 Y019 K000 / R209 G159 B167 / #D19FA7

C035 M018 Y002 K000 / R162 G183 B216 / #A2B7D8

C006 M015 Y038 K000 / R237 G209 B155 / #EDD19B

C009 M029 Y012 K000 / R225 G182 B191 / #E1BF6F

C075 M049 Y039 K013 / R057 G088 B102 / #395866

C018 M049 Y024 K000 / R197 G131 B143 / #C5838F

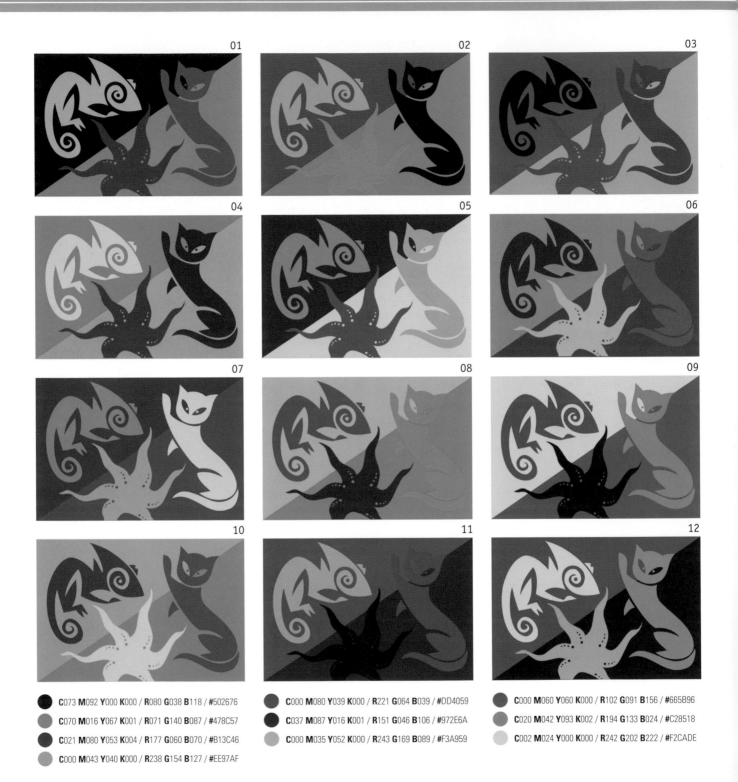

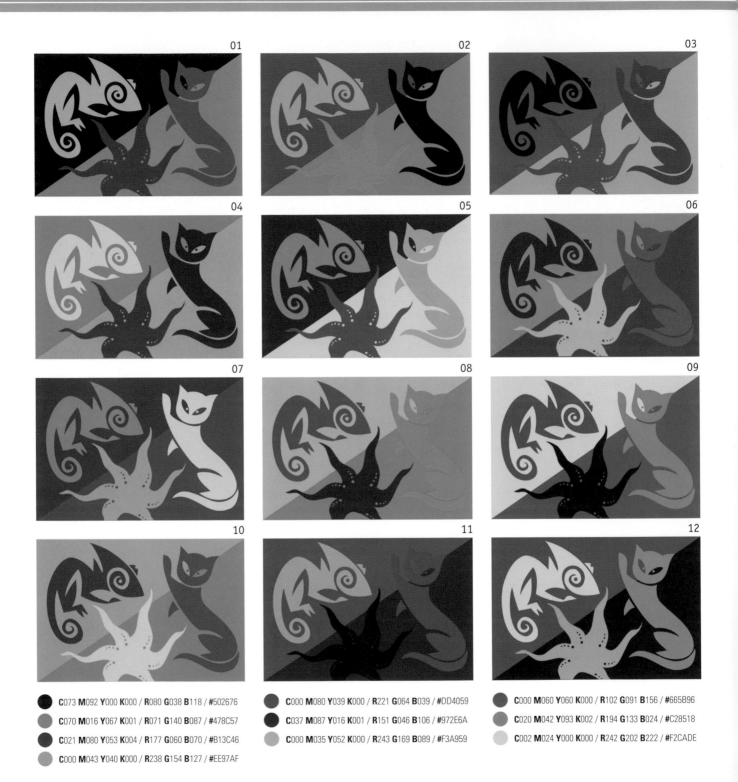 **C**073 **M**092 **Y**000 **K**000 / **R**080 **G**038 **B**118 / #502676

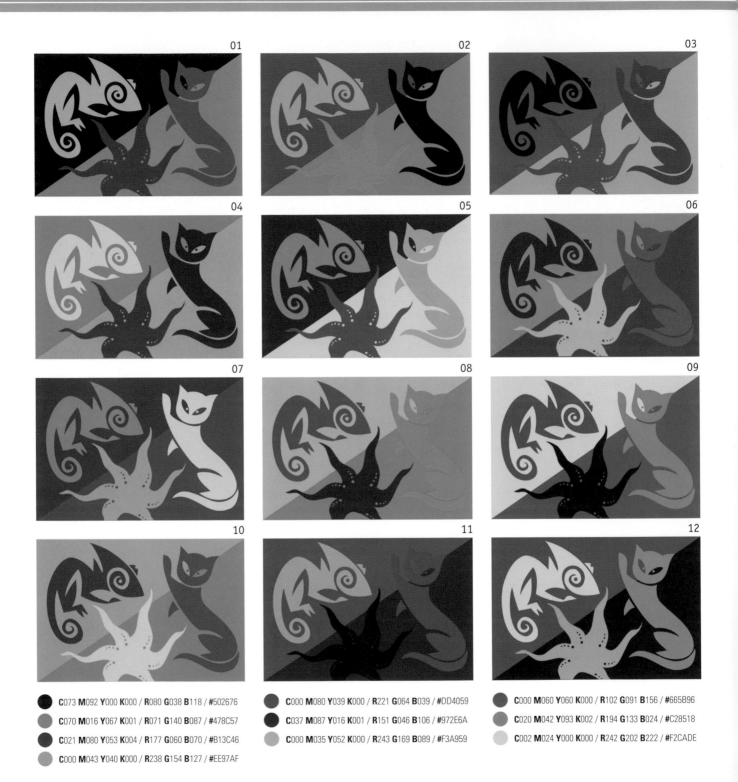 **C**070 **M**016 **Y**067 **K**001 / **R**071 **G**140 **B**087 / #478C57

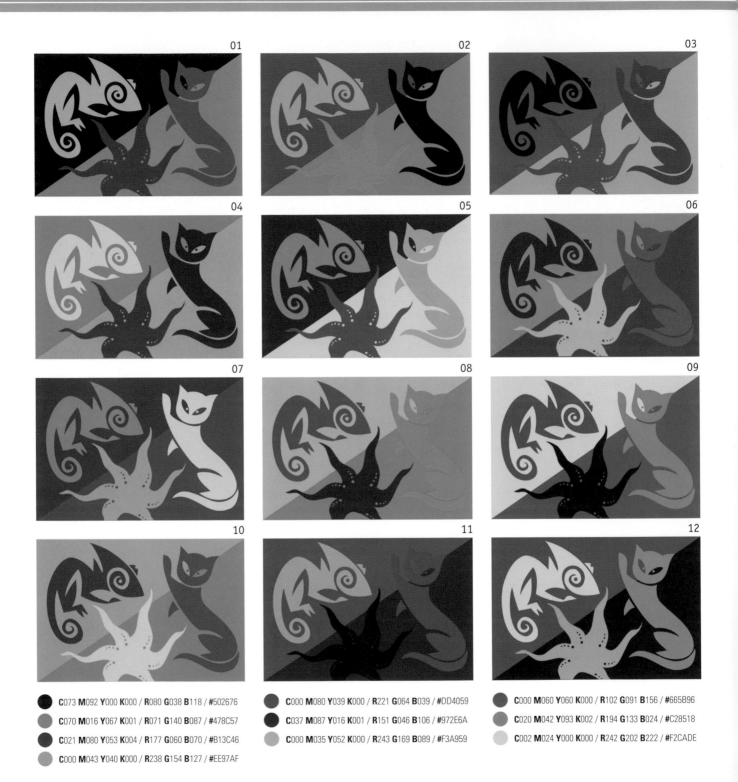 **C**021 **M**080 **Y**053 **K**004 / **R**177 **G**060 **B**070 / #B13C46

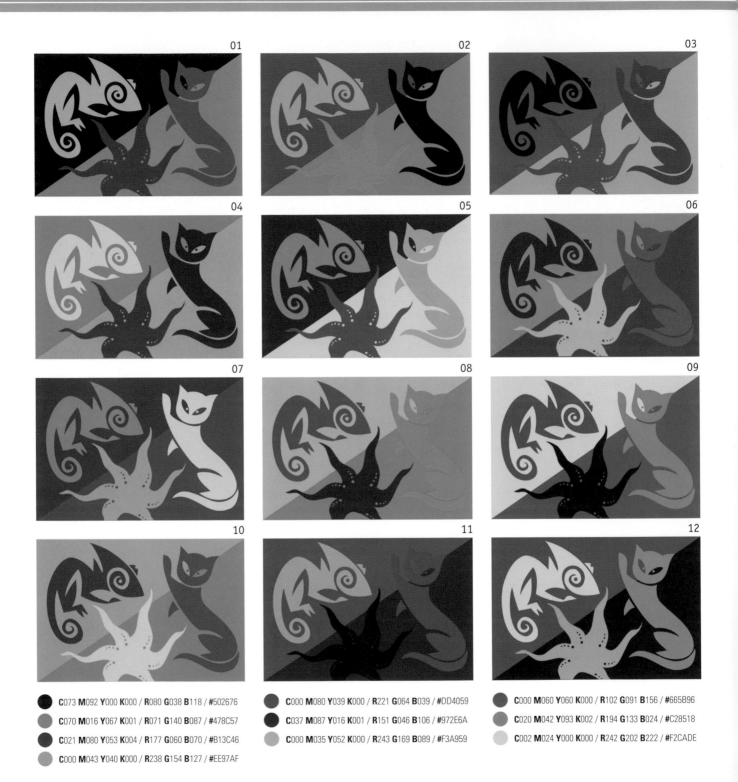 **C**000 **M**043 **Y**040 **K**000 / **R**238 **G**154 **B**127 / #EE97AF

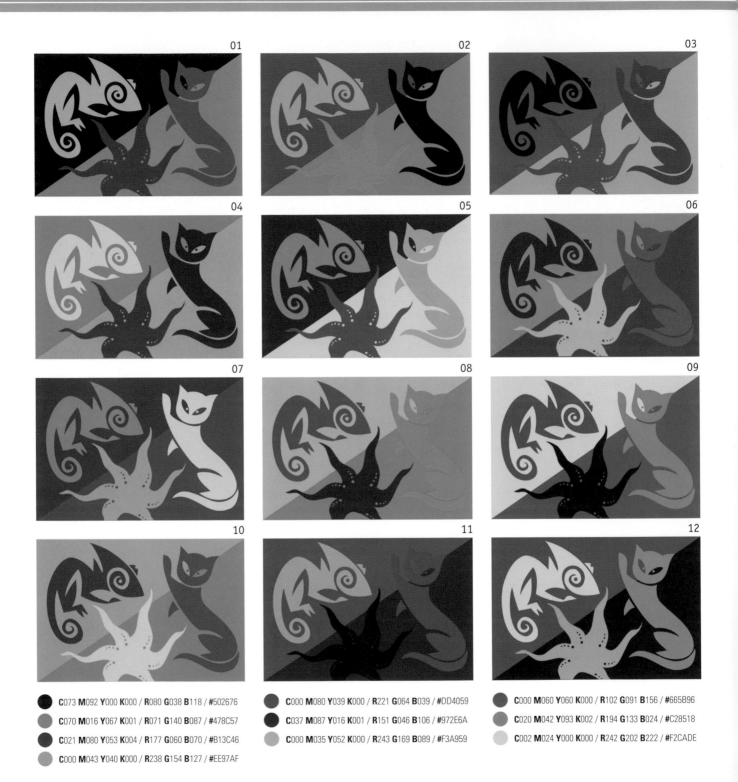 **C**000 **M**080 **Y**039 **K**000 / **R**221 **G**064 **B**039 / #DD4059

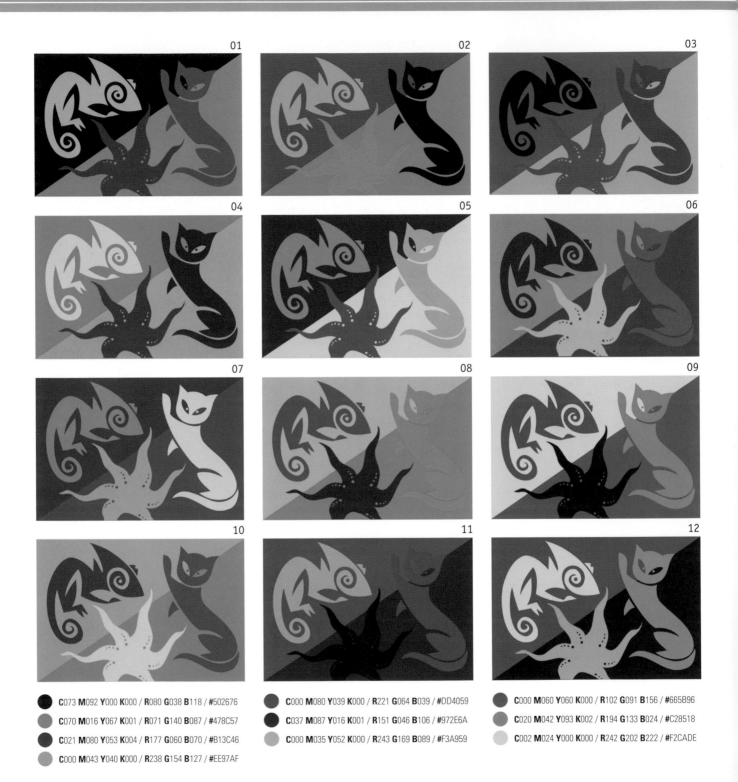 **C**037 **M**087 **Y**016 **K**001 / **R**151 **G**046 **B**106 / #972E6A

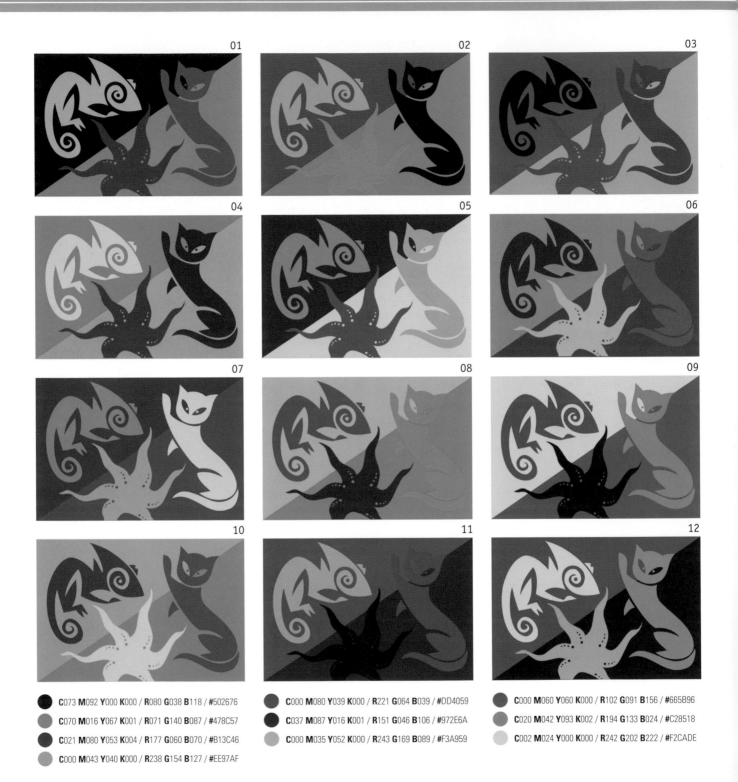 **C**000 **M**035 **Y**052 **K**000 / **R**243 **G**169 **B**089 / #F3A959

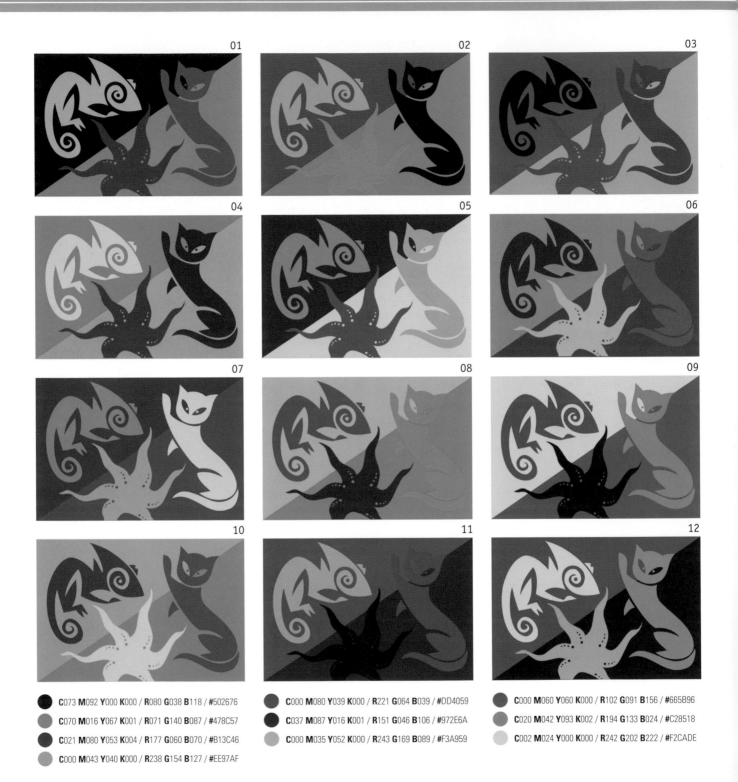 **C**000 **M**060 **Y**060 **K**000 / **R**102 **G**091 **B**156 / #665B96

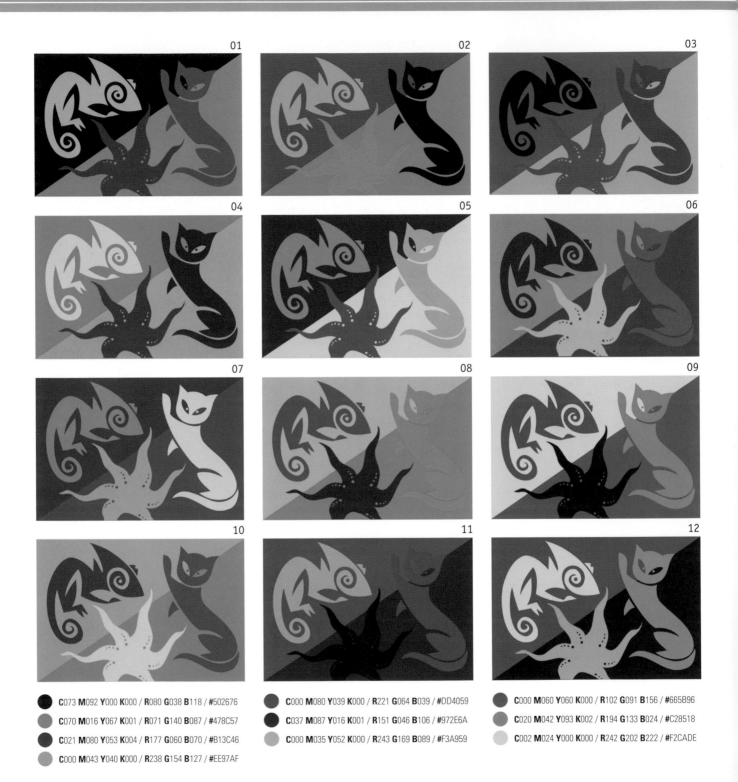 **C**020 **M**042 **Y**093 **K**002 / **R**194 **G**133 **B**024 / #C28518

 C002 **M**024 **Y**000 **K**000 / **R**242 **G**202 **B**222 / #F2CADE

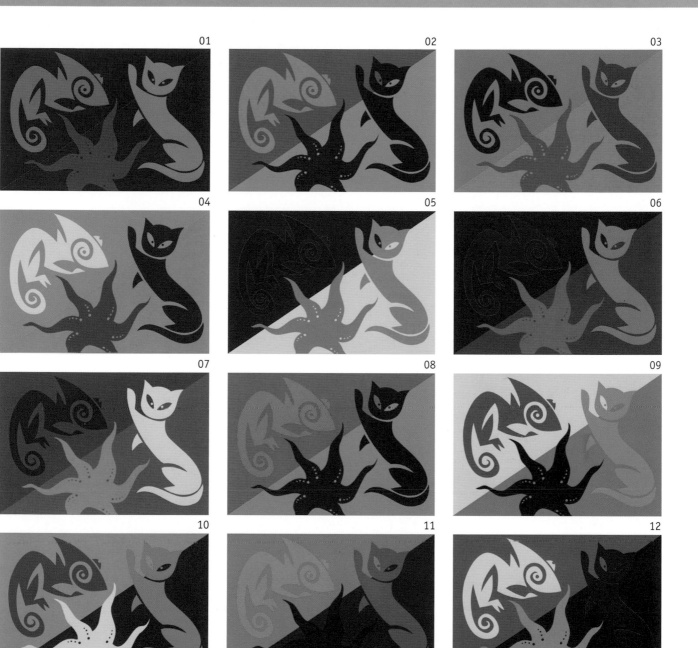

C089 M079 Y098 K001 / R039 G054 B122 / #27367A

C049 M023 Y090 K003 / R132 G144 B040 / #849028

C006 M024 Y008 K000 / R232 G197 B206 / #E8C5CE

C000 M056 Y006 K000 / R231 G126 B162 / #E77EA2

C011 M075 Y000 K000 / R202 G075 B137 / #CA4B89

C050 M084 Y000 K000 / R105 G051 B126 / #69337E

C000 M071 Y017 K000 / R225 G089 B125 / #E1597D

C059 M036 Y016 K000 / R101 G130 B164 / #6582A4

C017 M092 Y050 K002 / R184 G035 B068 / #B82344

C007 M022 Y000 K000 / R230 G201 B223 / #E6C9DF

Emotion and Attitude

01

02

03

04

05

06

07

08

09

10

11

12

C055 M021 Y100 K003 / R119 G141 B018 / #778D12

C005 M088 Y050 K000 / R210 G045 B071 / #D22D47

C076 M020 Y043 K000 / R036 G137 B165 / #2489A5

C000 M000 Y000 K090 / R049 G047 B048 / #2F2E30

C004 M093 Y100 K001 / R209 G031 B020 / #D11F14

C035 M001 Y093 K000 / R175 G193 B019 / #AFC113

C066 M000 Y033 K000 / R072 G171 B164 / #48ABA4

C021 M081 Y100 K010 / R166 G055 B020 / #A63714

C076 M016 Y044 K001 / R045 G139 B130 / #2D8B82

C039 M048 Y071 K015 / R135 G101 B059 / #87653B

C018 M100 Y100 K012 / R163 G013 B022 / #A30D16

C008 M031 Y045 K000 / R228 G174 B126 / #E4AE74

01 02 03
04 05 06
07 08 09
10 11 12

C019 M092 Y094 K003 / R179 G036 B028 / #B3241C

C082 M019 Y004 K000 / R000 G135 B197 / #0087C5

C027 M019 Y072 K000 / R191 G177 B075 / #BFB14B

C064 M063 Y070 K090 / R019 G017 B014 / #13110E

C094 M063 Y003 K001 / R000 G074 B145 / #004A91

C001 M085 Y087 K000 / R218 G053 B032 / #DA3520

C000 M017 Y062 K000 / R252 G205 B097 / #FCCD61

C094 M081 Y019 K010 / R024 G048 B101 / #183065

C015 M029 Y071 K001 / R214 G167 B072 / #D6A748

C036 M067 Y047 K015 / R136 G075 B079 / #884B4F

C094 M062 Y017 K012 / R000 G067 B117 / #004375

C033 M042 Y007 K000 / R165 G139 B176 / #A58BB0

This combination of twelve colors combines both discord and harmony. The reds, when juxtaposed with the greens and blues, are a potent combination, while the brown, beige, and gray tend to mute the color scheme. White space is a fundamental component and should always be factored in to any use of color. This palette is ideally suited to a magazine feature or a Web site.

09

03

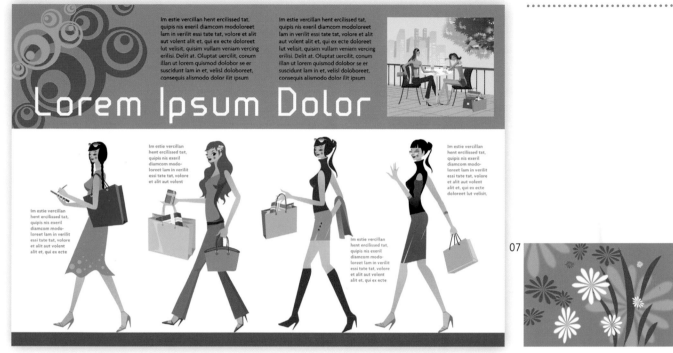

Lorem Ipsum Dolor

Im estie vercillan hent ercilissed tat, quipis nis exeril diamcom modoloreet lam in verilit essi tate tat, volore et alit aut volent alit et, qui ex ecte doloreet lut velisit, quisim vullam veniam vercing erilisi. Delit at. Oluptat uercilit, conum illan ut lorem quismod dolobor se er suscidunt lam in et, velisl doloboreet, consequis alismodo dolor ilit ipsum

Im estie vercillan hent ercilissed tat, quipis nis exeril diamcom modoloreet lam in verilit essi tate tat, volore et alit aut volent alit et, qui ex ecte doloreet lut velisit, quisim vullam veniam vercing erilisi. Delit at. Oluptat uercilit, conum illan ut lorem quismod dolobor se er suscidunt lam in et, velisl doloboreet, consequis alismodo dolor ilit ipsum

Im estie vercillan hent ercilissed tat, quipis nis exeril diamcom modoloreet lam in verilit essi tate tat, volore et alit aut volent

Im estie vercillan hent ercilissed tat, quipis nis exeril diamcom modoloreet lam in verilit essi tate tat, volore et alit aut volent

Im estie vercillan hent ercilissed tat, quipis nis exeril diamcom modoloreet lam in verilit essi tate tat, volore et alit aut volent alit et, qui ex ecte

Im estie vercillan hent ercilissed tat, quipis nis exeril diamcom modoloreet lam in verilit essi tate tat, volore et alit aut volent alit et, qui ex ecte doloreet lut velisit,

07

01

Lorem Ipsum Dolor

Im estie vercillan hent ercilissed tat, quipis nis exeril diamcom modoloreet lam in verilit essi tate tat, volore et alit aut volent alit et, qui ex ecte doloreet lut velisit, quisim vullam veniam vercing erilisi. Delit at. Oluptat uercilit, conum illan ut lorem quismod dolobor se er suscidunt lam in et, velisl doloboreet, consequis alismodo dolor ilit ipsum

Im estie vercillan hent ercilissed tat, quipis nis exeril diamcom modoloreet lam in verilit essi tate tat, volore et alit aut volent alit et, qui ex ecte doloreet lut velisit, quisim vullam veniam vercing erilisi. Delit at. Oluptat uercilit, conum illan ut lorem quismod dolobor se er suscidunt lam in et, velisl doloboreet, consequis alismodo dolor ilit ipsum

Im estie vercillan hent ercilissed tat, quipis nis exeril diamcom modoloreet lam in verilit essi tate tat, volore et alit aut volent

Im estie vercillan hent ercilissed tat, quipis nis exeril diamcom modoloreet lam in verilit essi tate tat, volore et alit aut volent alit et, qui ex ecte doloreet lut velisit,

Im estie vercillan hent ercilissed tat, quipis nis exeril diamcom modoloreet lam in verilit essi tate tat, volore et alit aut volent alit et, qui ex ecte

Im estie vercillan hent ercilissed tat, quipis nis exeril diamcom modoloreet lam in verilit essi tate tat, volore et alit aut volent alit et, qui ex ecte

01

02

03

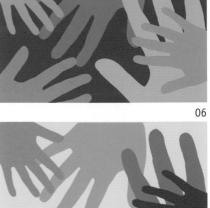

04

05

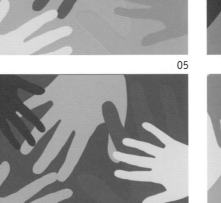

06

07

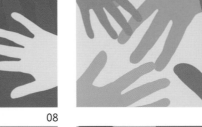

08

09

10

11

12

C059 M045 Y002 K000 / R101 G117 B175 / #6575AF

C059 M002 Y047 K000 / R099 G173 B134 / #63AD86

C041 M062 Y072 K001 / R148 G090 B059 / #945A3B

C000 M044 Y073 K000 / R239 G147 B061 / #EF933D

C013 M034 Y032 K000 / R215 G166 B148 / #D7A694

C073 M053 Y056 K000 / R074 G093 B087 / #4A5D57

C063 M003 Y001 K013 / R064 G157 B200 / #409DC8

C012 M045 Y056 K005 / R202 G133 B090 / #CA855A

C070 M072 Y040 K000 / R084 G067 B094 / #54435E

C000 M014 Y052 K000 / R253 G214 B123 / #FDD67B

C027 M021 Y058 K000 / R187 G175 B104 / #BBAF68

01

02

03

04

05

06

07

08

09

10

11

12

C049 **M**002 **Y**059 **K**000 / **R**133 **G**183 **B**110 / #85B76E

C002 **M**044 **Y**059 **K**000 / **R**234 **G**148 **B**089 / #EA9459

C060 **M**072 **Y**041 **K**000 / **R**105 **G**070 **B**093 / #69465D

C039 **M**073 **Y**000 **K**000 / **R**149 **G**074 **B**139 / #954A8B

C034 **M**034 **Y**013 **K**000 / **R**165 **G**154 **B**178 / #A59AB2

C053 **M**055 **Y**073 **K**000 / **R**124 **G**098 **B**062 / #7C623E

C007 **M**001 **Y**063 **K**013 / **R**214 **G**203 **B**090 / #D6CB5A

C042 **M**056 **Y**012 **K**005 / **R**137 **G**102 **B**142 / #89668E

C072 **M**040 **Y**068 **K**000 / **R**073 **G**109 **B**077 / #496D4D

C011 **M**052 **Y**000 **K**000 / **R**211 **G**132 **B**176 / #D384B0

C021 **M**058 **Y**030 **K**000 / **R**189 **G**110 **B**124 / #BD6E7C

01

02

03

04

05

06

07

08

09

10

11

12

C008 M000 Y032 K000 / R238 G239 B181 / #EEEFB5

C026 M036 Y000 K000 / R183 G157 B197 / #B79DC5

C033 M007 Y000 K000 / R167 G205 B234 / #A7CDEA

C000 M023 Y042 K000 / R248 G198 B141 / #F8C68D

C015 M023 Y000 K000 / R212 G193 B220 / #D4C1DC

C036 M000 Y026 K000 / R163 G208 B188 / #A3D0BC

C000 M004 Y035 K000 / R255 G240 B172 / #FFF0AC

C017 M000 Y015 K000 / R214 G233 B216 / #D6E9D8

C016 M000 Y034 K000 / R219 G229 B174 / #DBE5AE

C031 M018 Y000 K000 / R173 G188 B222 / #ADBCDE

C037 M046 Y000 K000 / R156 G129 B181 / #9C81B5

C017 M006 Y000 K000 / R210 G225 B242 / #D2E1F2

01

02

03

04

05

06

07

08

09

10

11

12

C000 **M**010 **Y**027 **K**000 / **R**253 **G**228 **B**183 / #FDE4B7

C047 **M**027 **Y**000 **K**000 / **R**131 **G**157 **B**205 / #839DCD

C034 **M**000 **Y**000 **K**000 / **R**167 **G**217 **B**243 / #A7D9F3

C001 **M**036 **Y**036 **K**000 / **R**239 **G**168 **B**139 / #EFA98B

C028 **M**024 **Y**000 **K**000 / **R**180 **G**181 **B**215 / #B4B5D7

C023 **M**000 **Y**022 **K**000 / **R**199 **G**224 **B**199 / #C7E0C7

C000 **M**020 **Y**030 **K**000 / **R**249 **G**207 **B**168 / #F9CFA8

C009 **M**003 **Y**0013 **K**000 / **R**232 **G**236 **B**220 / #E8ECDC

C002 **M**004 **Y**030 **K**000 / **R**251 **G**238 **B**183 / #FBEEB7

C039 **M**007 **Y**000 **K**000 / **R**152 **G**200 **B**233 / #98C8E9

C063 **M**027 **Y**000 **K**000 / **R**083 **G**142 **B**200 / #538EC8

C019 **M**007 **Y**000 **K**000 / **R**206 **G**220 **B**239 / #CEDCEF

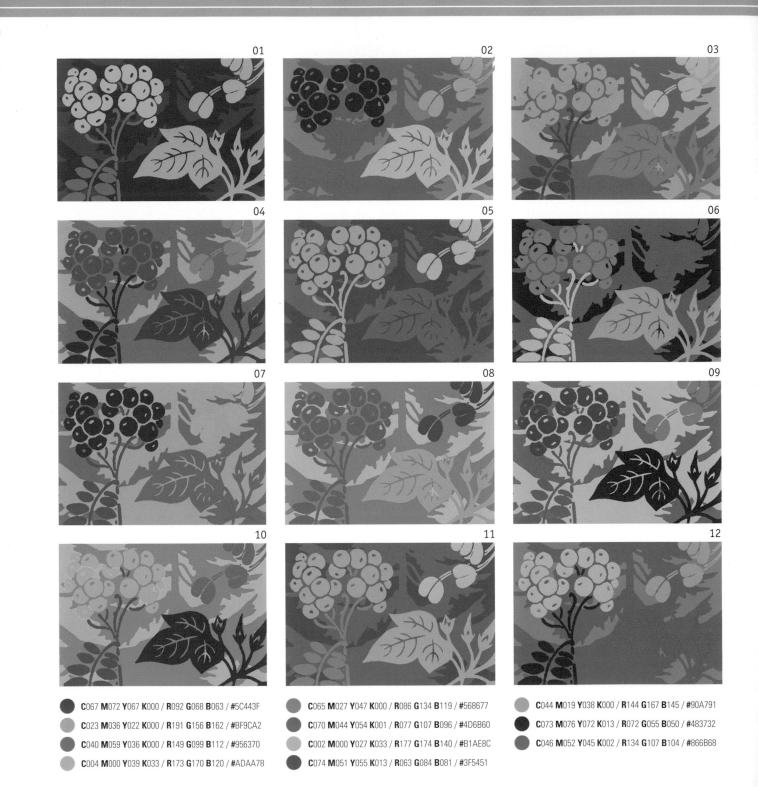

C067 M072 Y067 K000 / R092 G068 B063 / #5C443F

C023 M036 Y022 K000 / R191 G156 B162 / #BF9CA2

C040 M059 Y036 K000 / R149 G099 B112 / #956370

C004 M000 Y039 K033 / R173 G170 B120 / #ADAA78

C065 M027 Y047 K000 / R086 G134 B119 / #568677

C070 M044 Y054 K001 / R077 G107 B096 / #4D6B60

C002 M000 Y027 K033 / R177 G174 B140 / #B1AE8C

C074 M051 Y055 K013 / R063 G084 B081 / #3F5451

C044 M019 Y038 K000 / R144 G167 B145 / #90A791

C073 M076 Y072 K013 / R072 G055 B050 / #483732

C046 M052 Y045 K002 / R134 G107 B104 / #866B68

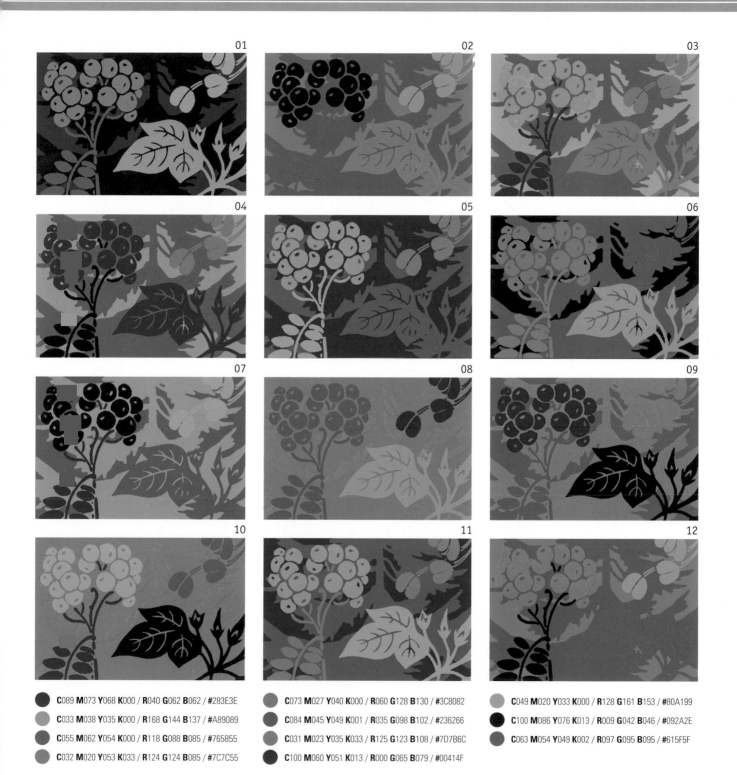

01 02 03
04 05 06
07 08 09
10 11 12

C089 **M**073 **Y**068 **K**000 / **R**040 **G**062 **B**062 / #283E3E

C033 **M**038 **Y**035 **K**000 / **R**168 **G**144 **B**137 / #A89089

C055 **M**062 **Y**054 **K**000 / **R**118 **G**088 **B**085 / #765855

C032 **M**020 **Y**053 **K**033 / **R**124 **G**124 **B**085 / #7C7C55

C073 **M**027 **Y**040 **K**000 / **R**060 **G**128 **B**130 / #3C8082

C084 **M**045 **Y**049 **K**001 / **R**035 **G**098 **B**102 / #236266

C031 **M**023 **Y**035 **K**033 / **R**125 **G**123 **B**108 / #7D7B6C

C100 **M**060 **Y**051 **K**013 / **R**000 **G**065 **B**079 / #00414F

C049 **M**020 **Y**033 **K**000 / **R**128 **G**161 **B**153 / #80A199

C100 **M**086 **Y**076 **K**013 / **R**009 **G**042 **B**046 / #092A2E

C063 **M**054 **Y**049 **K**002 / **R**097 **G**095 **B**095 / #615F5F

This is a palette of twelve opaque, low-key colors. The moody, sombre hues do not include any accent colors, instead there are lighter tonal variations of most colors. In these four options the colorways help create a suitable mood for the repeated zombie-like figures. Use this palette for print or screen, preferably without photographic subject matter, like this dust jacket for a novel.

01

02

07

09

01

02

03

04

05

06

07

08

09

10

11

12

C051 M047 Y000 K000 / R122 G119 B176 / #7A77B0

C049 M004 Y050 K000 / R130 G181 B129 / #82B581

C061 M024 Y001 K000 / R088 G149 B204 / #5895CC

C055 M017 Y038 K000 / R114 G159 B144 / #729F90

C005 M070 Y002 K000 / R216 G089 B143 / #D8598F

C000 M049 Y045 K000 / R236 G140 B112 / #EC8C70

C029 M059 Y051 K001 / R172 G102 B092 / #AC665C

C022 M049 Y007 K010 / R173 G119 B153 / #AD7799

C015 M036 Y049 K000 / R210 G158 B114 / #D29E72

C008 M015 Y062 K000 / R235 G202 B096 / #EBCA60

C035 M028 Y024 K000 / R164 G144 B155 / #A4909B

C000 M056 Y031 K000 / R232 G124 B125 / #E87C7D

01

02

03

04

05

06

07

08

09

10

11

12

C000 M051 Y050 K000 / R234 G133 B100 / #EA8564
C044 M045 Y009 K000 / R141 G126 B167 / #8D7EA7
C002 M060 Y034 K000 / R227 G112 B117 / #E37075
C031 M051 Y021 K000 / R170 G121 B144 / #AA7990

C002 M003 Y070 K000 / R255 G299 B078 / #FFE54E
C047 M000 Y049 K000 / R136 G190 B135 / #88BE87
C053 M029 Y059 K001 / R123 G139 B096 / #7B8B60
C008 M021 Y049 K010 / R210 G176 B115 / #D2B073

C049 M015 Y034 K000 / R130 G169 B156 / #82A99C
C062 M008 Y001 K000 / R081 G168 B201 / #51A8C9
C024 M033 Y038 K000 / R190 G159 B137 / #BE9F89
C034 M000 Y056 K000 / R174 G204 B119 / #AECC77

69

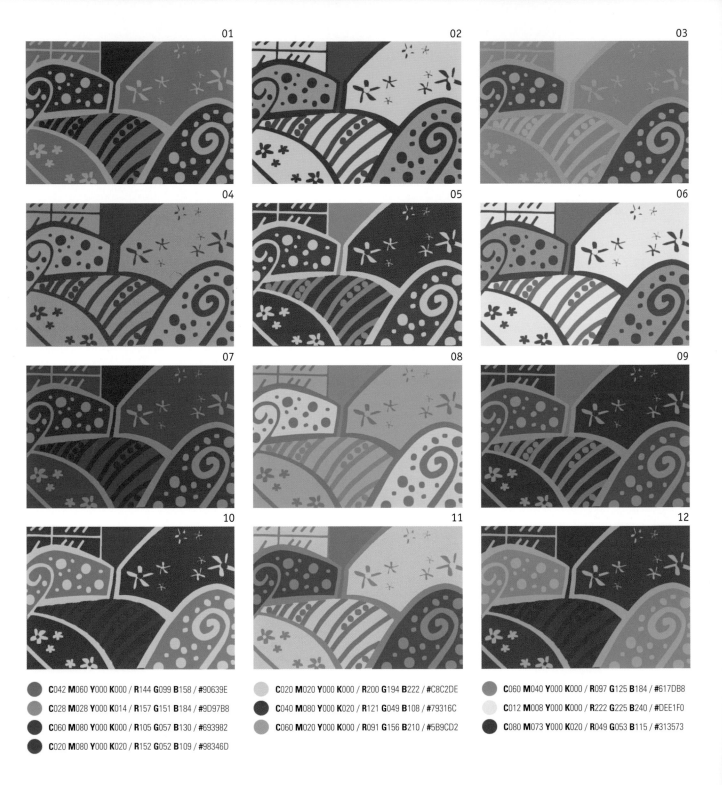

C042 M060 Y000 K000 / R144 G099 B158 / #90639E

C028 M028 Y000 K014 / R157 G151 B184 / #9D97B8

C060 M080 Y000 K000 / R105 G057 B130 / #693982

C020 M080 Y000 K020 / R152 G052 B109 / #98346D

C020 M020 Y000 K000 / R200 G194 B222 / #C8C2DE

C040 M080 Y000 K020 / R121 G049 B108 / #79316C

C060 M020 Y000 K000 / R091 G156 B210 / #5B9CD2

C060 M040 Y000 K000 / R097 G125 B184 / #617DB8

C012 M008 Y000 K000 / R222 G225 B240 / #DEE1F0

C080 M073 Y000 K020 / R049 G053 B115 / #313573

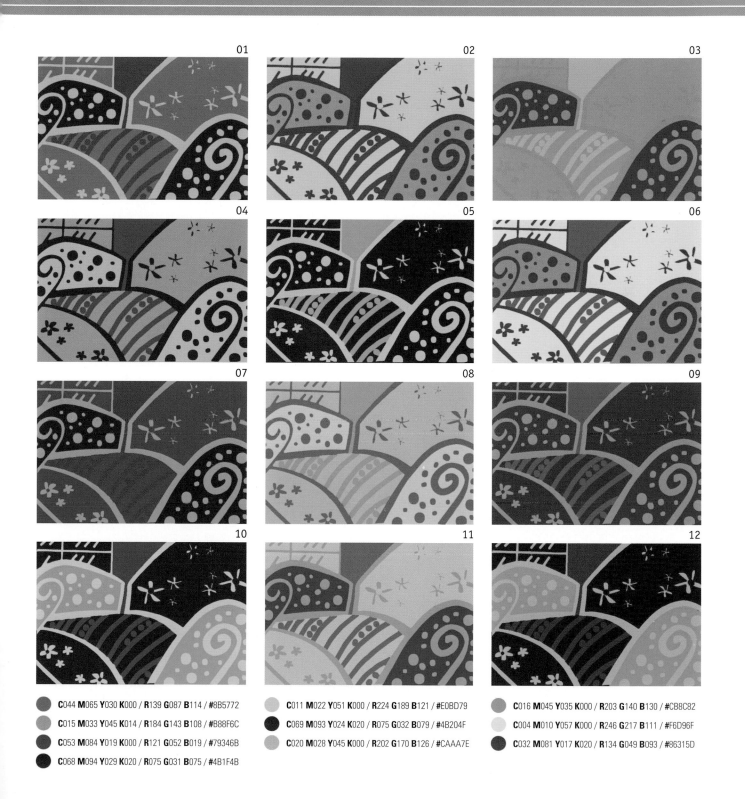

C044 M065 Y030 K000 / R139 G087 B114 / #8B5772

C015 M033 Y045 K014 / R184 G143 B108 / #B88F6C

C053 M084 Y019 K000 / R121 G052 B019 / #79346B

C068 M094 Y029 K020 / R075 G031 B075 / #4B1F4B

C011 M022 Y051 K000 / R224 G189 B121 / #E0BD79

C069 M093 Y024 K020 / R075 G032 B079 / #4B204F

C020 M028 Y045 K000 / R202 G170 B126 / #CAAA7E

C016 M045 Y035 K000 / R203 G140 B130 / #CB8C82

C004 M010 Y057 K000 / R246 G217 B111 / #F6D96F

C032 M081 Y017 K020 / R134 G049 B093 / #86315D

01

02

03

04

05

06

07

08

09

10

11

12

C028 M011 Y000 K000 / R180 G0203 B231 / #B4CBE7

C000 M032 Y020 K000 / R243 G182 B174 / #F3B6AE

C000 M010 Y017 K000 / R253 G231 B207 / #FDE7CF

C027 M011 Y001 K007 / R172 G192 B216 / #ACC0D8

C060 M018 Y001 K000 / R090 G158 B211 / #5A9ED3

C039 M055 Y004 K000 / R150 G110 B160 / #966EA0

C016 M037 Y004 K000 / R205 G161 B193 / #CDA1C1

C000 M002 Y005 K004 / R245 G239 B232 / #F5EFE8

C002 M025 Y004 K000 / R242 G199 B213 / #F2C7D5

C002 M036 Y009 K003 / R230 G168 B183 / #E6A8B7

C000 M021 Y025 K000 / R248 G205 B178 / #F8CDB2

C048 M027 Y004 K000 / R128 G156 B199 / #809CC7

01

02

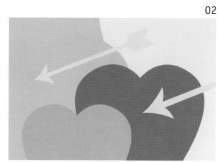

03

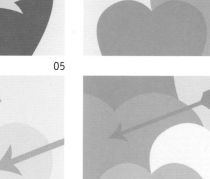

04

05

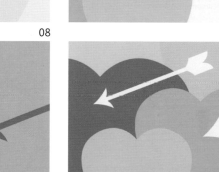

06

07

08

09

10

11

12

C007 **M**015 **Y**004 **K**000 / **R**232 **G**216 **B**225 / #E8D8D1

C000 **M**042 **Y**010 **K**000 / **R**238 **G**160 **B**178 / #EEA0B2

C000 **M**013 **Y**009 **K**000 / **R**251 **G**226 **B**219 / #FBE2DB

C007 **M**015 **Y**004 **K**005 / **R**222 **G**207 **B**215 / #DECFD7

C016 **M**024 **Y**004 **K**000 / **R**210 **G**189 **B**210 / #D2BDD2

C010 **M**073 **Y**005 **K**000 / **R**205 **G**081 **B**135 / #CD5187

C004 **M**049 **Y**005 **K**000 / **R**226 **G**141 **B**174 / #E28DAE

C000 **M**003 **Y**005 **K**002 / **R**249 **G**242 **B**234 / #F9F2EA

C001 **M**033 **Y**005 **K**000 / **R**241 **G**183 **B**200 / #F1B7C8

C001 **M**047 **Y**007 **K**001 / **R**232 **G**145 **B**173 / #E891AD

C000 **M**028 **Y**011 **K**000 / **R**244 **G**192 **B**196 / #F4C0C4

C013 **M**035 **Y**005 **K**000 / **R**214 **G**168 **B**194 / #D6A8C2

This palette includes variants of the classic boy-girl colors of pink and blue along with creams and purples. The result is a twelve-color pastel set that is versatile, but with a distinctly feminine bias. The low-key colors are particularly suited to cosmetics advertising, women's magazine features, or, as here, a teaser for a romantic television soap opera.

04

05

Im estie vercillan hent ercilissed tat, quipis nis exeril diamcom modoloreet lam in verilit essi tate tat volore et alit aut volent alit et qui ex ecte doloreet lut velisit quisim vullam veniam vercing erilisi Delit atluptat uercilit conum illan ut lorem quismod dolobor se er suscidunt lam in et velisl doloboreet consequis alismodo dolor ilit ipsum dolorper sequisi. Dunt alis adignis dolobor perat velis el dolorpe rcillandrem ver si. Guer sed magna ad dignim el iurer se molestrud et ing er si

Im estie vercillan hent ercilissed tat, quipis nis exeril diamcom modoloreet lam in verilit essi tate tat volore et alit aut volent alit et qui ex ecte doloreet lut velisit quisim vullam veniam vercing erilisi Delit atluptal uercilit conum illan ut lorem quismod dolobor se er suscidunt lam in et velisl doloboreet consequis alismodo dolor ilit ipsum dolorper sequisi. Dunt alis adignis dolobor perat velis el dolorpe rcillandrem ver si. Guer sed magna ad dignim el iurer se molestrud et ing er si

Im estie vercillan hent ercilissed tat, quipis nis exeril diamcom modoloreet lam in verilit essi tate tat volore et alit aut volent alit et qui ex ecte doloreet lut velisit quisim vullam veniam vercing erilisi Delit atluptat uercilit conum illan ut lorem quismod dolobor se er suscidunt lam in et velisl doloboreet consequis alismodo dolor ilit ipsum dolorper sequisi. Dunt alis adignis dolobor perat velis el dolorpe rcillandrem ver si. Guer sed magna ad dignim el iurer se molestrud et ing er si

09

11

Im estie vercillan hent ercilissed tat, quipis nis exeril diamcom modoloreet lam in verilit essi tate tat volore et alit aut volent alit et qui ex ecte doloreet lut velisit quisim vullam veniam vercing erilisi Delit atluptat uercilit conum illan ut lorem quismod dolobor se er suscidunt lam in et velisl doloboreet consequis alismodo dolor ilit ipsum dolorper sequisi. Dunt alis adignis dolobor perat velis el dolorpe rcillandrem ver si. Guer sed magna ad dignim el iurer se molestrud et ing er si

01

02

03

04

05

06

07

08

09

10
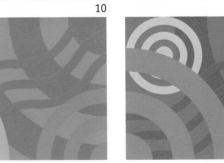

11

12

- C059 M006 Y002 K039 / R059 G116 B146 / #3B7492
- C063 M020 Y002 K000 / R082 G153 B206 / #5299CE
- C084 M006 Y037 K004 / R000 G139 B144 / #008B90
- C077 M000 Y025 K000 / R000 G160 B177 / #00A0B1

- C051 M007 Y010 K000 / R118 G184 B210 / #76B8D2
- C025 M002 Y000 K010 / R174 G205 B224 / #AECDE0
- C070 M004 Y012 K002 / R045 G163 B199 / #2DA3C7
- C064 M020 Y030 K009 / R079 G136 B144 / #4F8890

- C028 M017 Y035 K000 / R185 G187 B156 / #B9BB9C
- C030 M003 Y004 K000 / R177 G215 B233 / #B1D7E9
- C062 M041 Y014 K000 / R093 G121 B162 / #5D79A2
- C056 M000 Y006 K000 / R097 G188 B223 / #61BCDF

01 02 03
04 05 06
07 08 09
10 11 12

● C066 M000 Y060 K039 / R051 G110 B073 / #336E49

● C052 M000 Y048 K000 / R121 G185 B136 / #79B988

● C064 M000 Y026 K004 / R072 G168 B174 / #48A8AE

● C057 M000 Y035 K000 / R102 G181 B163 / #66B5A3

○ C028 M000 Y042 K000 / R188 G214 B153 / #BCD699

○ C011 M000 Y028 K010 / R210 G216 B174 / #D2D8AE

● C047 M000 Y059 K002 / R137 G185 B110 / #89B96E

● C054 M000 Y037 K009 / R104 G171 B147 / #68AB93

○ C003 M000 Y020 K000 / R249 G247 B209 / #F9F7D1

○ C008 M000 Y018 K000 / R238 G242 B213 / #EEF2D5

● C052 M000 Y022 K000 / R115 G190 B193 / #73BEC1

● C028 M000 Y051 K000 / R190 G212 B131 / #BED483

This palette uses colors of similar tonal value and intensity. The result is largely monochromatic and is best suited to subject matter where sheer impact is not of overriding concern. Here, the exercise photos use the Luminosity Layer Blending Mode so that they inherit the background color, while their shadows, which are on a separate layer, use Multiply as their Blending Mode.

01

04

Lorem

Im estie vercillan hent ercilissed tat, quipis nis exeril diamcom modoloree lam in verilit essi tate tat, volore et alit aut volent alit et, qui ex ecte doloreet

1

2

3

4

5

6

7

8

9

Im estie vercillan hent ercilissed tat, quipis nis exeril diamcom modoloreet lam in verilit essi tate tat, volore et alit aut volent alit et, qui ex ecte doloreet lut velisit, quisim vullam veniam vercino erilisi. 1 elit at luptat uercilit, conum illan ut lorem quismod dolobor se er suscidunt 2 lam in et, velisl doloboreet, consequis alismodo 3 dolor ilit ipsum dolorper sequisi. Dunt alis adignis 4 dolobor perat, velis el dolorpe scillandrem ver si. Guer sed magna 5 ad dignim el irmer se molestrud et ing er si blaor 6 lobore velit lorper suscipisl il utpate ver sequi 7 bla facidunt lametum in hent il ipis acing euipisl utem veliqui psuscidunt- 8 irilisissi. Nulla feugiatis ea am vel dipsum ad minibh et vullan henim ing. Im estie 9 vercillan hent ercilissed tat, quipis nis exeril diamcom modoloreet lam in verilit essi tate tat, volore et alit aut volent alit et, qui ex ecte doloreet lut velisit, quisim

Lorem

Im estie vercillan hent ercilissed tat, quipis nis exeril diamcom modoloree lam in verilit essi tate tat, volore et alit aut volent alit et, qui ex ecte doloreet

1

2

3

4

5

6

7

8

9

Im estie vercillan hent ercilissed tat, quipis nis exeril diamcom modoloreet lam in verilit essi tate tat, volore et alit aut volent alit et, qui ex ecte doloreet lut velisit, quisim vullam veniam vercing erilisi. 1 elit at luptat uercilit, conum illan ut lorem quismod dolobor se er suscidunt 2 lam in et, velisl doloboreet, consequis alismodo 3 dolor ilit ipsum dolorper sequisi. Dunt alis adignis 4 dolobor perat, velis el dolorpe rcillandrem ver si. Guer sed magna 5 ad dignim el irmer se molestrud et ing er si blaor 6 lobore velit lorper suscipisl il utpate ver sequi 7 bla facidunt lametum in hent il ipis acing euipisl utem veliqui psuscidunt- 8 irilisisi. Nulla feugatis ea am vel dipsum ad minibh et vullan henim ing. Im estie 9 vercillan hent ercilissed tat, quipis nis exeril diamcom modoloreet lam in verilit essi tate tat, volore et alit aut volent alit et, qui ex ecte doloreet lut velisit, quisim

Lorem

Im estie vercillan hent ercilissed tat, quipis nis exeril diamcom modoloreet lam in verilit essi tate tat, volore et alit aut volent alit et, qui ex ecte doloreet lut velisit, quisim vullam veniam vercing erilisi. 1 elit at luptat uercilit, conum illan ut lorem quismod dolobor se er suscidunt 2 lam in et, velisit doloboreet, consequis alismodu 3 dolor ilit ipsum dolorper sequisi. Dunt alis adignis 4 dolobor perat, velis el dolorpe rcillandrem ver si. Guer sed magna 5 ad dignim el jurer se molestrud et ing et si blaor 6 lobore velit lorper suscipisl il utpate ver sequi 7 bla facidunt lametum in hent il ipis acing euipisl utem veliqui psuscidunt 8 irilisissi. Nulla feugiatis ea am vel dipsum ad minibh et vullan henim ing. Im estie 9 vercillan hent ercilissed tat, quipis nis exeril diamcom modoloreet lam in verilit essi tate tat, volore et alit aut volent alit et, qui ex ecte doloreet lut velisit, quisim

1 Im estie vercillan hent ercilissed tat, quipis nis exeril diamcom modoloree lam in verilit essi tate tat, volore et alit aut volent alit et, qui ex ecte doloreet

5 Im estie vercillan hent ercilissed tat, quipis nis exeril diacom modoloreet lam in verilit essi tate tat, volore et alit aut volent alit et, qui ex ecte doloreet lut velisit, quisim vullam

05

Lorem

Im estie vercillan hent ercilissed tat, quipis nis exeril diamcom modoloreet lam in verilit essi tate tat, volore et alit aut volent alit et, qui ex ecte doloreet lut velisit, quisim vullan veniam vercing erilisi. 1 elit at luptat uercilit, conum illan ut lorem quismod dolobor se er suscidunt 2 lam in et, velisit doloboreet, consequis alismodo 3 dolor ilit ipsum dolorper sequisi. Dunt alis adignis 4 dolobor perat, velis el dolorpe rcillandrem ver si. Guer sed magna 5 ad dignim el jurer se molestrud et ing et si blaor 6 lobore velit lorper suscipisl il utpate ver sequi 7 bla facidunt lametum in hent il ipis acing euipisl utem veliqui psuscidunt 8 irilisissi. Nulla feugiatis ea am vel dipsum ad minibh et vullan henim ing. Im estie 9 vercillan hent ercilissed tat, quipis nis exeril diamcom modoloreet lam in verilit essi tate tat, volore et alit aut volent alit et, qui ex ecte doloreet lut velisit, quisim

1 Im estie vercillan hent ercilissed tat, quipis nis exeril diamcom modoloree lam in verilit essi tate tat, volore et alit aut volent alit et, qui ex ecte doloreet

5 Im estie vercillan hent ercilissed tat, quipis nis exeril diacom modoloreet lam in verilit essi tate tat, volore et alit aut volent alit et, qui ex ecte doloreet lut velisit, quisim vullam

09

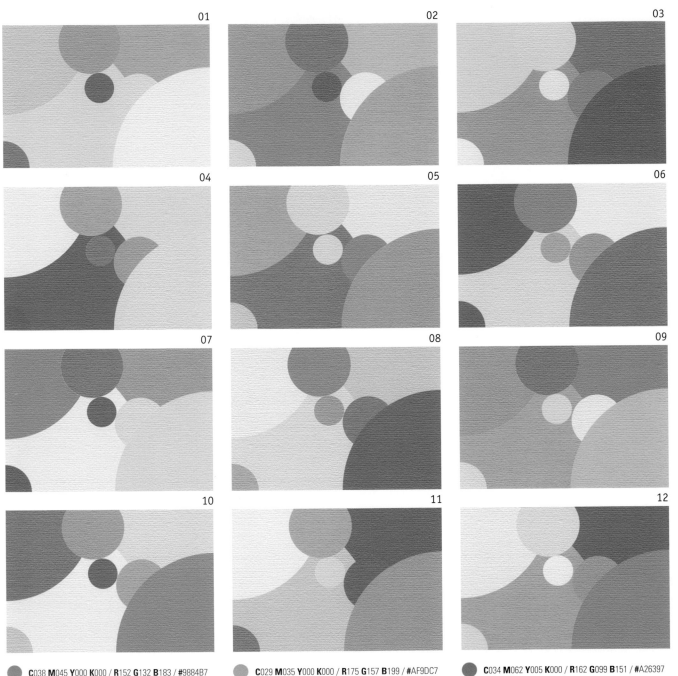

01

02

03

04

05

06

07

08

09

10

11

12

C038 M045 Y000 K000 / R152 G132 B183 / #9884B7

C017 M023 Y001 K000 / R206 G191 B218 / #CEBFDA

C040 M014 Y010 K000 / R150 G185 B205 / #96B9CD

C005 M013 Y024 K000 / R239 G218 B188 / #EFDABC

C029 M035 Y000 K000 / R175 G157 B199 / #AF9DC7

C013 M009 Y003 K000 / R220 G223 B233 / #DCDFE9

C007 M012 Y036 K000 / R234 G198 B153 / #EAC699

C062 M029 Y020 K000 / R090 G138 B165 / #5A8AA5

C034 M062 Y005 K000 / R162 G099 B151 / #A26397

C009 M011 Y002 K000 / R230 G223 B233 / #E6DFE9

C015 M032 Y068 K000 / R213 G163 B077 / #D5A34D

C027 M038 Y082 K003 / R180 G137 B049 / #B48931

01 02 03
04 05 06
07 08 09
10 11 12

C045 M000 Y039 K000 / R142 G195 B157 / #8EC39D

C023 M001 Y018 K000 / R199 G225 B209 / #C7E1D1

C013 M010 Y040 K000 / R223 G212 B152 / #DFD498

C013 M024 Y005 K000 / R216 G192 B209 / #D8C0D1

C035 M000 Y030 K000 / R168 G209 B180 / #A8D1B4

C009 M003 Y013 K000 / R234 G236 B220 / #EAECDC

C021 M036 Y007 K000 / R194 G160 B188 / #C2A0BC

C028 M020 Y062 K000 / R186 G174 B095 / #BAAE5F

C062 M005 Y035 K000 / R089 G169 B159 / #59A99F

C011 M002 Y009 K000 / R228 G236 B230 / #E4ECE6

C033 M068 Y016 K000 / R162 G086 B129 / #A25681

C039 M082 Y027 K003 / R144 G056 B098 / #903862

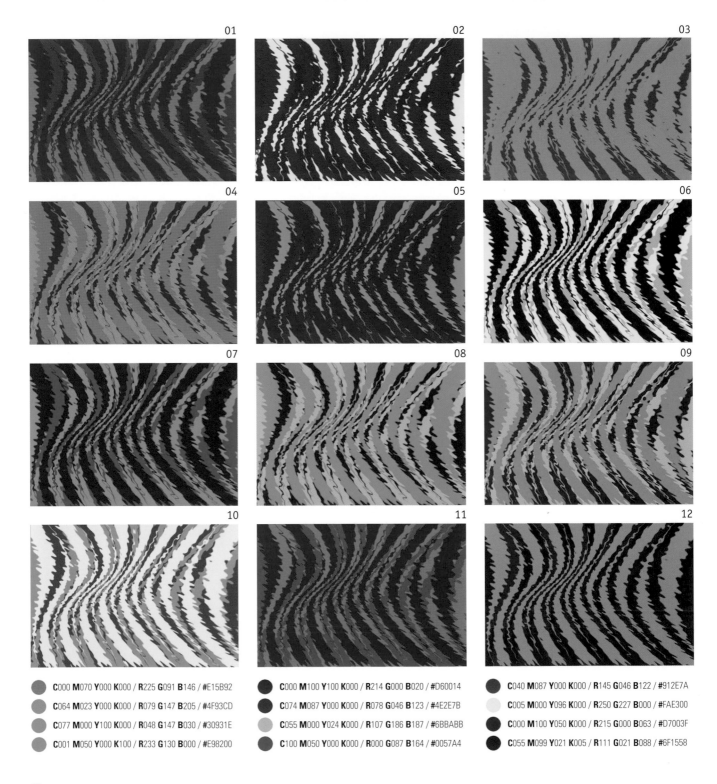

C000 M070 Y000 K000 / R225 G091 B146 / #E15B92

C064 M023 Y000 K000 / R079 G147 B205 / #4F93CD

C077 M000 Y100 K000 / R048 G147 B030 / #30931E

C001 M050 Y000 K100 / R233 G130 B000 / #E98200

C000 M100 Y100 K000 / R214 G000 B020 / #D60014

C074 M087 Y000 K000 / R078 G046 B123 / #4E2E7B

C055 M000 Y024 K000 / R107 G186 B187 / #6BBABB

C100 M050 Y000 K000 / R000 G087 B164 / #0057A4

C040 M087 Y000 K000 / R145 G046 B122 / #912E7A

C005 M000 Y096 K000 / R250 G227 B000 / #FAE300

C000 M100 Y050 K000 / R215 G000 B063 / #D7003F

C055 M099 Y021 K005 / R111 G021 B088 / #6F1558

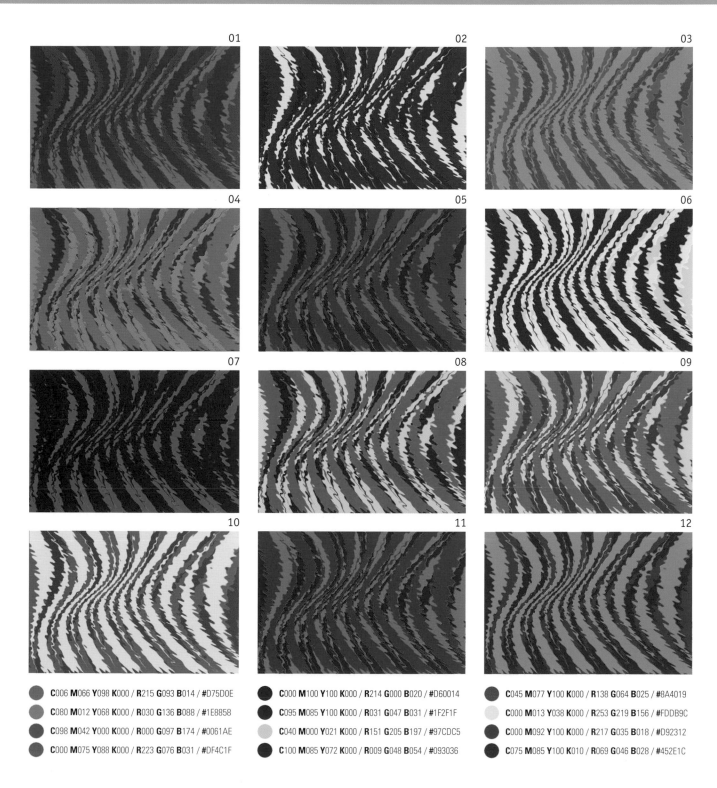

C006 M066 Y098 K000 / R215 G093 B014 / #D75D0E
C080 M012 Y068 K000 / R030 G136 B088 / #1E8858
C098 M042 Y000 K000 / R000 G097 B174 / #0061AE
C000 M075 Y088 K000 / R223 G076 B031 / #DF4C1F

C000 M100 Y100 K000 / R214 G000 B020 / #D60014
C095 M085 Y100 K000 / R031 G047 B031 / #1F2F1F
C040 M000 Y021 K000 / R151 G205 B197 / #97CDC5
C100 M085 Y072 K000 / R009 G048 B054 / #093036

C045 M077 Y100 K000 / R138 G064 B025 / #8A4019
C000 M013 Y038 K000 / R253 G219 B156 / #FDDB9C
C000 M092 Y100 K000 / R217 G035 B018 / #D92312
C075 M085 Y100 K010 / R069 G046 B028 / #452E1C

01

02

03

04

05

06

07

08

09

10

11

12

C047 M000 Y013 K000 / R129 G198 B213 / #81C6D5

C000 M018 Y027 K000 / R250 G212 B176 / #FAD4B0

C000 M042 Y001 K013 / R208 G143 B171 / #D08FAB

C011 M000 Y014 K029 / R169 G178 B166 / #A9B2A6

C000 M042 Y003 K000 / R237 G161 B189 / #EDA1BD

C033 M025 Y000 K000 / R168 G174 B212 / #A8AED4

C035 M002 Y000 K045 / R097 G127 B145 / #617F91

C014 M030 Y000 K045 / R125 G107 B126 / #7D6B7E

C011 M000 Y015 K008 / R211 G222 B203 / #D3DECB

C000 M035 Y016 K000 / R241 G175 B177 / #F1AFB1

01

02

03

04

05
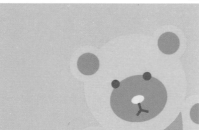

06

07

08

09

10

11
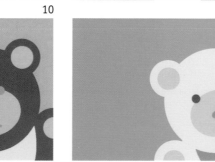

12

C062 **M**023 **Y**007 **K**000 / **R**086 **G**149 **B**194 / #5695C2

C011 **M**009 **Y**021 **K**000 / **R**226 **G**220 **B**197 / #E2DCC5

C004 **M**052 **Y**028 **K**009 / **R**208 **G**122 **B**125 / #D07A7D

C011 **M**001 **Y**007 **K**026 / **R**175 **G**185 **B**183 / #AFB9B7

C002 **M**052 **Y**027 **K**000 / **R**229 **G**132 **B**137 / #E58489

C016 **M**033 **Y**003 **K**000 / **R**207 **G**171 **B**200 / #CFABC8

C042 **M**021 **Y**002 **K**051 / **R**079 **G**095 **B**117 / #4F5F75

C007 **M**038 **Y**008 **K**052 / **R**120 **G**089 **B**102 / #785966

C012 **M**001 **Y**008 **K**005 / **R**215 **G**228 **B**223 / #D7E4DF

C001 **M**033 **Y**031 **K**000 / **R**241 **G**178 **B**153 / #F1B299

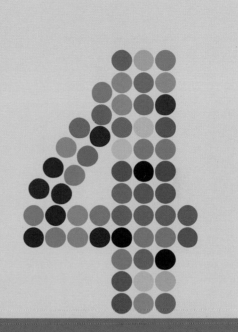

Natural Affinity

01

02

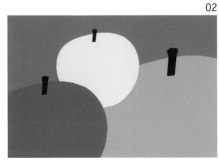

03

04

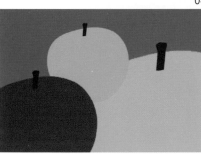

05

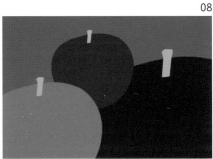

06

07

08

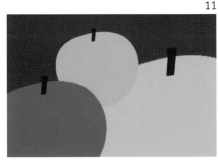

09

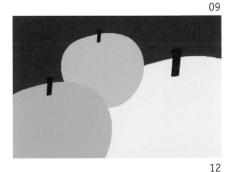

10

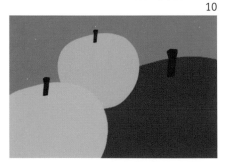

11

12

C011 M023 Y089 K000 / R226 G180 B026 / #E2B41A

C009 M075 Y100 K001 / R205 G074 B014 / #CD4A0E

C011 M000 Y051 K000 / R233 G231 B133 / #E9E785

C025 M060 Y029 K001 / R179 G104 B121 / #B36879

C009 M065 Y097 K001 / R210 G095 B017 / #D25F11

C025 M020 Y095 K000 / R196 G173 B006 / #C4AD06

C013 M075 Y056 K001 / R197 G073 B072 / #C54948

C031 M088 Y056 K017 / R139 G039 B057 / #8B2739

C022 M100 Y100 K017 / R148 G015 B022 / #940F16

C013 M033 Y092 K000 / R217 G159 B021 / #D99F15

C013 M095 Y096 K004 / R187 G027 B025 / #BB1B19

C033 M093 Y065 K033 / R112 G037 B040 / #701B28

01

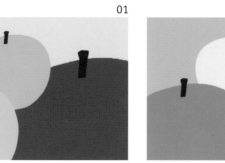

02

03

04

05

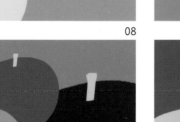

06

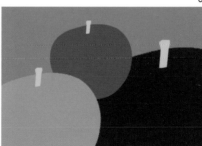

07

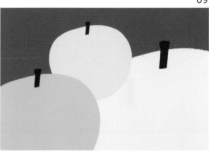

08

09

10

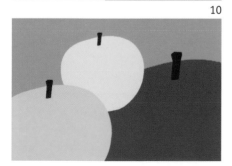

11

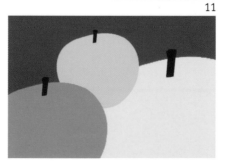

12

C013 M000 Y096 K000 / R232 G219 B000 / #E8DB00

C018 M048 Y100 K002 / R198 G124 B000 / #C67C00

C009 M000 Y052 K000 / R238 G233 B129 / #EEE981

C022 M044 Y046 K001 / R181 G138 B112 / #BF8A70

C022 M017 Y100 K000 / R205 G180 B000 / #CCB400

C033 M000 Y100 K000 / R181 G196 B000 / #B5C400

C015 M057 Y068 K001 / R200 G110 B066 / #C86E42

C036 M067 Y078 K030 / R115 G061 B038 / #733D26

C031 M091 Y100 K040 / R105 G029 B018 / #691D12

C018 M000 Y100 K000 / R220 G213 B000 / #DCD500

C020 M077 Y100 K009 / R171 G062 B019 / #AB3E13

C036 M084 Y087 K051 / R084 G031 B023 / #541F17

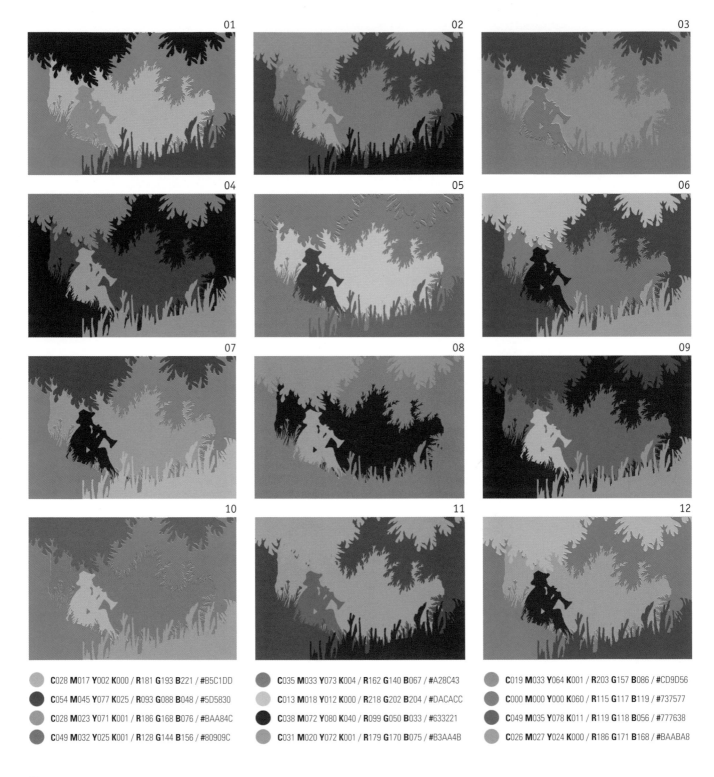

C028 M017 Y002 K000 / R181 G193 B221 / #B5C1DD

C054 M045 Y077 K025 / R093 G088 B048 / #5D5830

C028 M023 Y071 K001 / R186 G168 B076 / #BAA84C

C049 M032 Y025 K001 / R128 G144 B156 / #80909C

C035 M033 Y073 K004 / R162 G140 B067 / #A28C43

C013 M018 Y012 K000 / R218 G202 B204 / #DACACC

C038 M072 Y080 K040 / R099 G050 B033 / #633221

C031 M020 Y072 K001 / R179 G170 B075 / #B3AA4B

C019 M033 Y064 K001 / R203 G157 B086 / #CD9D56

C000 M000 Y000 K060 / R115 G117 B119 / #737577

C049 M035 Y078 K011 / R119 G118 B056 / #777638

C026 M027 Y024 K000 / R186 G171 B168 / #BAABA8

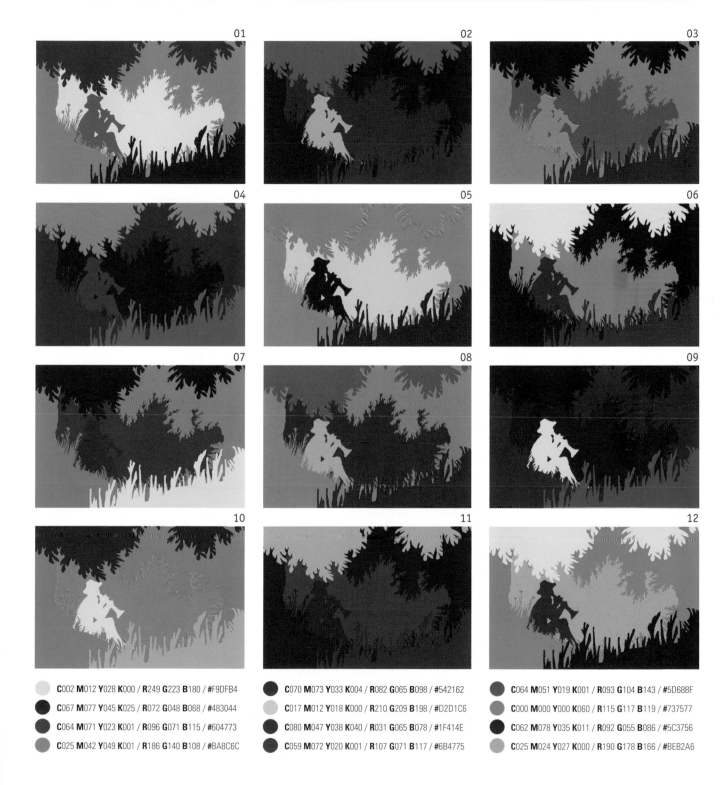

C002 M012 Y028 K000 / R249 G223 B180 / #F9DFB4
C067 M077 Y045 K025 / R072 G048 B068 / #483044
C064 M071 Y023 K001 / R096 G071 B115 / #604773
C025 M042 Y049 K001 / R186 G140 B108 / #BA8C6C

C070 M073 Y033 K004 / R082 G065 B098 / #542162
C017 M012 Y018 K000 / R210 G209 B198 / #D2D1C6
C080 M047 Y038 K040 / R031 G065 B078 / #1F414E
C059 M072 Y020 K001 / R107 G071 B117 / #6B4775

C064 M051 Y019 K001 / R093 G104 B143 / #5D688F
C000 M000 Y000 K060 / R115 G117 B119 / #737577
C062 M078 Y035 K011 / R092 G055 B086 / #5C3756
C025 M024 Y027 K000 / R190 G178 B166 / #BEB2A6

This is a much simplified version of a palette that painter John Constable might have used. The hues are naturalistic and evoke the rustic charm of times past. However the colors are well suited to a contemporary interpretation, like packaging for an eco-friendly product, a Web site for an environmental organization, or this leaflet for a country park.

02

04

Lorem Ipsum Dolor

Im estie vercillan hent ercilised tat, quipis nis exeril diamcom modoloreet lam in verilit essi tate tat, volore et alit aut volent alit et qui ex ecte doloreet lut velisit quisi vullam veniam vercing erilisi. Delit at. Oluptat uercilit conum illan ut lorem quismod dolobor se er suscidunt lam in et velisi doloboreet consequi alismodo dolor ilit ipsum dolorper sequisi. Dunt alis adignis dolobor perat, velis el dolorpe rcil-

Vercillan hent ercilised tat, quipis nis exeril diamcom modoloreet lam in verilit essi tate tat volore et alit aut volent alit et qui ex ecte doloree lut velisit quisim vullam veniam vercing eril Delit at Oluptat uerci litconum illan ut lorem quismod dolobor se er suscidunt lam in et, velisl doloboreet consequis alismo dolor ilit ipsum dolorper sequisi. Dunt alis adignis dolobor perat velis el dolorpe rcillandrem ver si.

Lorem Ipsum Dolor

Im estie vercillan hent ercilised tat, quipis nis exeril diamcom modoloreet lam in verilit essi tate tat, volore et alit aut volent alit et qui ex ecte doloreet lut velisit quisi vullam veniam vercing erilisi. Delit at. Oluptat uercilit conum illan ut lorem quismod dolobor se er suscidunt lam in et velisl doloboreet consequi alismodo dolor ilit ipsum dolorper sequisi. Dunt alis adignis dolobor perat, velis el dolorpe rcil-

Vercillan hent ercilised tat, quipis nis exeril diamcom modoloreet lam in verilit essi tate tat volore et alit aut volent alit et qui ex ecte doloree lut velisit quisim vullam veniam vercing eril Delit at Oluptat uerci litconum illan ut lorem quismod dolobor se er suscidunt lam in et, velisl doloboreet consequis alismo dolor ilit ipsum dolorper sequisi. Dunt alis adignis dolobor perat velis el dolorpe rcillandrem ver si.

Lorem Ipsum Dolor

Im estie vercillan hent ercilissed tat, quipis nis exeril diamcom modoloreet lam in verilit essi tate tat, volore et alit aut volent alit et qui ex ecte doloreet lot velisit quisi vullam veniam vercing erilisi. Delit at. Oluptat uercilit conum illan ut lorem quismod dolobor se er suscidunt lam in et velisl doloboreet consequi alismodo dolor ilit ipsum dolorper sequisi. Dunt alis adignis dolobor perat, velis el dolorpe rcil-

Vercillan hent ercilissed tat, quipis nis exeril diamcom modoloreet lam in verilit essi tate tat volore et alit aut volent alit et qui ex ecte doloree lut velisit quisim vullam veniam vercing eril Delit at Oluptat uerci litconum illan ut lorem quismod dolobor se er suscidunt lam in et, velisl doloboreet consequis alismo dolor ilit ipsum dolorper sequisi. Dunt alis adignis dolobor perat velis el dolorpe rcillandrem ver si.

08

09

Lorem Ipsum Dolor

tat, quipis nis exeril diamcom modoloreet lam in verilit essi tate tat, volore et alit aut volent alit et qui ex ecte doloreet lot velisit quisi vullam veniam vercing erilisi. Delit at. Oluptat uercilit conum illan ut lorem quismod dolobor se er suscidunt lam in et velisl doloboreet consequi alismodo dolor ilit ipsum dolorper sequisi. Dunt alis adignis dolobor perat, velis el dolorpe rcil-

nis exeril diamcom modoloreet lam in verilit essi tate tat volore et alit aut volent alit et qui ex ecte doloree lut velisit quisim vullam veniam vercing eril Delit at Oluptat uerci litconum illan ut lorem quismod dolobor se er suscidunt lam in et, velisl doloboreet consequis alismo dolor ilit ipsum dolorper sequisi. Dunt alis adignis dolobor perat velis el dolorpe rcillandrem ver si.

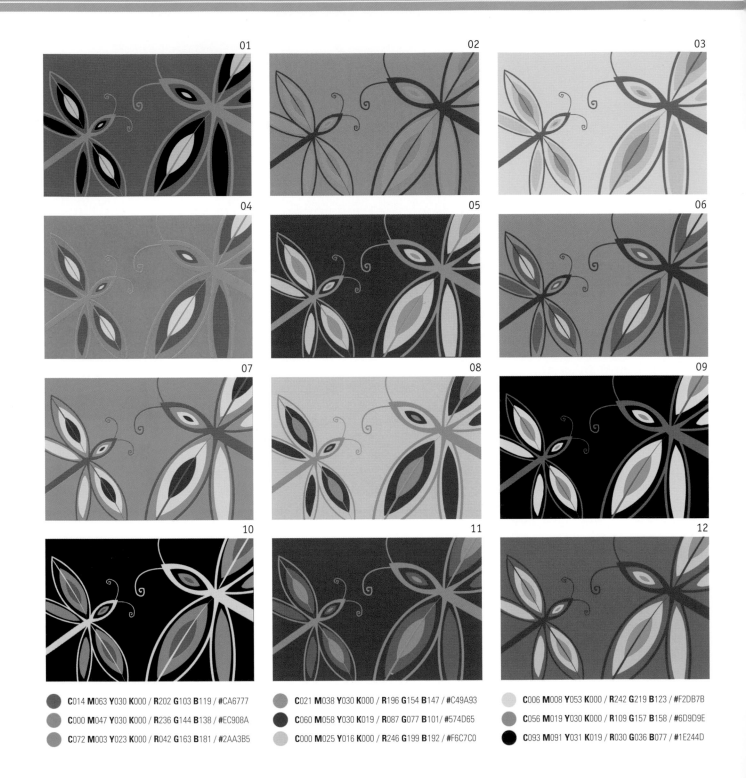

C014 M063 Y030 K000 / R202 G103 B119 / #CA6777

C000 M047 Y030 K000 / R236 G144 B138 / #EC908A

C072 M003 Y023 K000 / R042 G163 B181 / #2AA3B5

C021 M038 Y030 K000 / R196 G154 B147 / #C49A93

C060 M058 Y030 K019 / R087 G077 B101 / #574D65

C000 M025 Y016 K000 / R246 G199 B192 / #F6C7C0

C006 M008 Y053 K000 / R242 G219 B123 / #F2DB7B

C056 M019 Y030 K000 / R109 G157 B158 / #6D9D9E

C093 M091 Y031 K019 / R030 G036 B077 / #1E244D

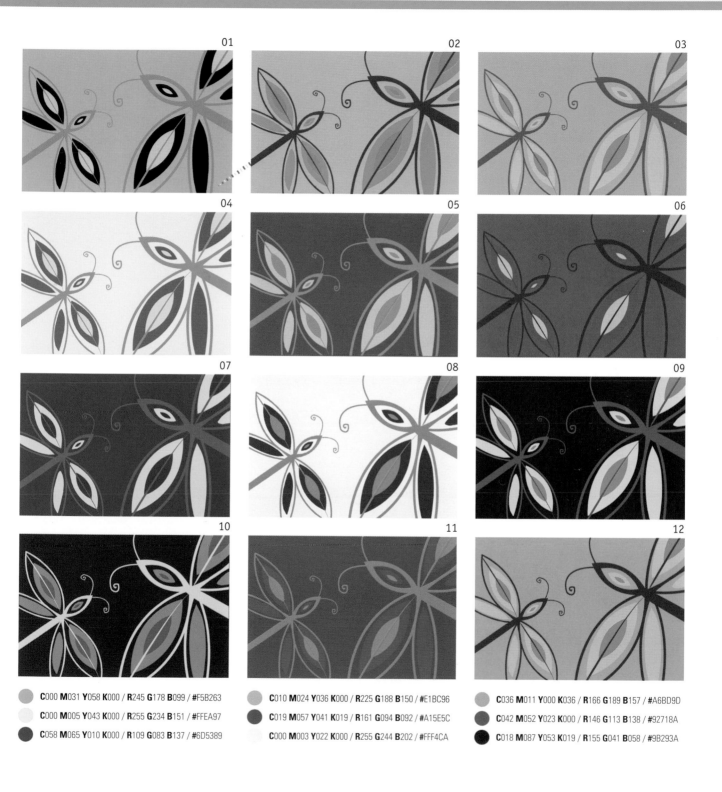

C000 M031 Y058 K000 / R245 G178 B099 / #F5B263

C000 M005 Y043 K000 / R255 G234 B151 / #FFEA97

C058 M065 Y010 K000 / R109 G083 B137 / #6D5389

C010 M024 Y036 K000 / R225 G188 B150 / #E1BC96

C019 M057 Y041 K019 / R161 G094 B092 / #A15E5C

C000 M003 Y022 K000 / R255 G244 B202 / #FFF4CA

C036 M011 Y000 K036 / R166 G189 B157 / #A6BD9D

C042 M052 Y023 K000 / R146 G113 B138 / #92718A

C018 M087 Y053 K019 / R155 G041 B058 / #9B293A

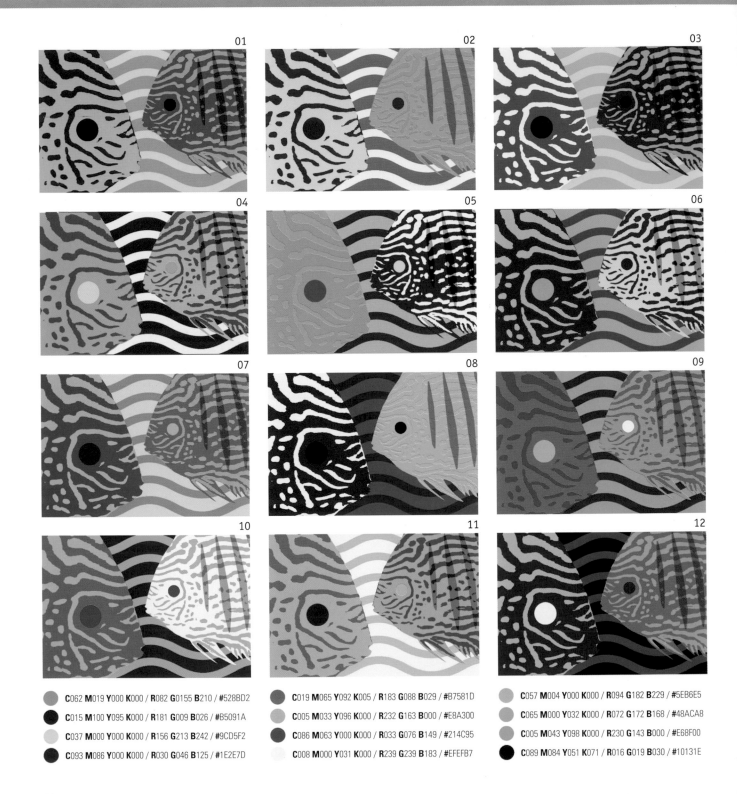

01 02 03
04 05 06
07 08 09
10 11 12

C062 M019 Y000 K000 / R082 G0155 B210 / #528BD2

C015 M100 Y095 K000 / R181 G009 B026 / #B5091A

C037 M000 Y000 K000 / R156 G213 B242 / #9CD5F2

C093 M086 Y000 K000 / R030 G046 B125 / #1E2E7D

C019 M065 Y092 K005 / R183 G088 B029 / #B7581D

C005 M033 Y096 K000 / R232 G163 B000 / #E8A300

C086 M063 Y000 K000 / R033 G076 B149 / #214C95

C008 M000 Y031 K000 / R239 G239 B183 / #EFEFB7

C057 M004 Y000 K000 / R094 G182 B229 / #5EB6E5

C065 M000 Y032 K000 / R072 G172 B168 / #48ACA8

C005 M043 Y098 K000 / R230 G143 B000 / #E68F00

C089 M084 Y051 K071 / R016 G019 B030 / #10131E

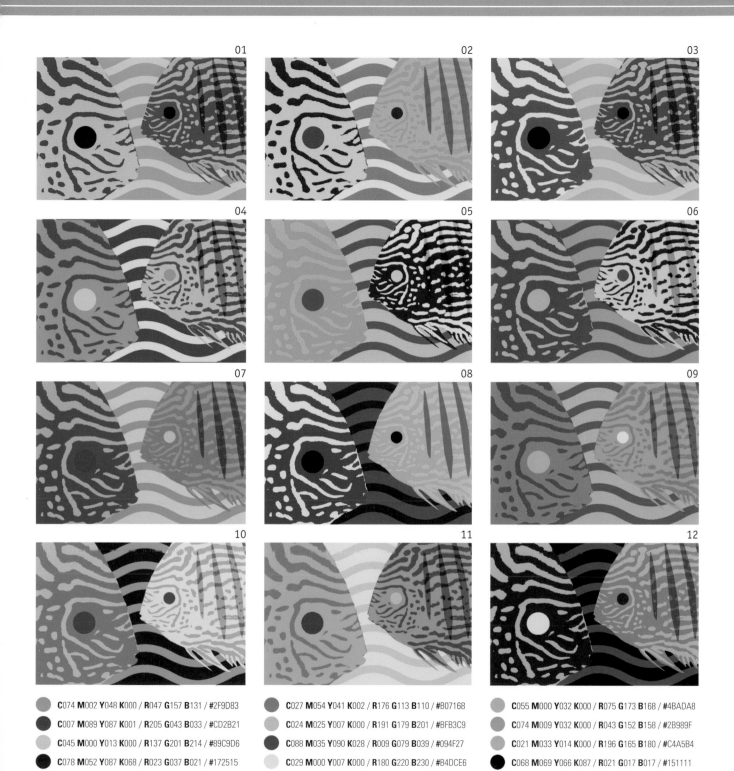

01 02 03
04 05 06
07 08 09
10 11 12

C074 **M**002 **Y**048 **K**000 / **R**047 **G**157 **B**131 / #2F9D83

C007 **M**089 **Y**087 **K**001 / **R**205 **G**043 **B**033 / #CD2B21

C045 **M**000 **Y**013 **K**000 / **R**137 **G**201 **B**214 / #89C9D6

C078 **M**052 **Y**087 **K**068 / **R**023 **G**037 **B**021 / #172515

C027 **M**054 **Y**041 **K**002 / **R**176 **G**113 **B**110 / #B07168

C024 **M**025 **Y**007 **K**000 / **R**191 **G**179 **B**201 / #BFB3C9

C088 **M**035 **Y**090 **K**028 / **R**009 **G**079 **B**039 / #094F27

C029 **M**000 **Y**007 **K**000 / **R**180 **G**220 **B**230 / #B4DCE6

C055 **M**000 **Y**032 **K**000 / **R**075 **G**173 **B**168 / #4BADA8

C074 **M**009 **Y**032 **K**000 / **R**043 **G**152 **B**158 / #2B989F

C021 **M**033 **Y**014 **K**000 / **R**196 **G**165 **B**180 / #C4A5B4

C068 **M**069 **Y**066 **K**087 / **R**021 **G**017 **B**017 / #151111

01
02
03

04
05
06

07
08
09

10
11
12

C073 M056 Y062 K000 / R074 G088 B077 / #4A584D

C018 M062 Y013 K000 / R194 G103 B142 / #C2678E

C071 M016 Y018 K000 / R055 G148 B178 / #3794B2

C048 M064 Y041 K000 / R132 G088 B101 / #845865

C060 M011 Y005 K000 / R088 G167 B210 / #58A7D2

C066 M071 Y056 K011 / R084 G064 B070 / #544046

C060 M032 Y005 K000 / R096 G137 B187 / #6089BB

C062 M017 Y013 K012 / R078 G148 B169 / #4E8CA9

01

02

03

04

05

06

07

08

09

10

11

12

C042 **M**056 **Y**084 **K**034 / **R**103 **G**070 **B**034 / #674622

C038 **M**040 **Y**074 **K**000 / **R**159 **G**130 **B**065 / #9F8241

C020 **M**037 **Y**081 **K**000 / **R**201 **G**147 **B**050 / #C99332

C058 **M**061 **Y**078 **K**008 / **R**102 **G**080 **B**050 / #675032

C079 **M**080 **Y**082 **K**016 / **R**058 **G**048 **B**040 / #3A3028

C016 **M**020 **Y**072 **K**000 / **R**215 **G**185 **B**073 / #D7B949

This unusual combination of colors contrasts the darker muted tones of green, red, and blue with a garish blue and magenta. The result can be slightly disturbing when used with graphics derived from mythological creatures. This palette should be used when legibility is not the first consideration—for example a CD sleeve or the cover of a modern art catalog.

09

10

Lorem Ipsum Doloron

Im estie vercillan hent ercilissed tat, quipis nis exeril diamcom modoloreet lam in verilit essi tate tat, volore et alit aut volent alit et, qui ex ecte doloreet lut velisit, quisim vullam veniam vercing erilisi. Delit at. Oluptat uercilit, conum illan ut lorem quismod dolobor se er suscidunt lam in et, velisl doloboreet, consequis alismodo dolor ilit ipsum dolorper sequisi. Dunt alis adignis dolobor perat, velis el

Lorem Ipsum Doloron

Im estie vercillan hent ercilissed tat, quipis nis exeril diamcom modoloreet lam in verilit essi tate tat, volore et alit aut volent alit et, qui ex ecte doloreet lut velisit, quisim vullam veniam vercing erilisi. Delit at. Oluptat uercilit, conum illan ut lorem quismod dolobor se er suscidunt lam in et, velisl doloboreet, consequis alismodo dolor ilit ipsum dolorper sequisi. Dunt alis adignis dolobor perat, velis el

Lorem Ipsum Doloron

Im estie vercillan hent encilissed tat, quipis nis exeril diamcom modoloreet lam in verilit essi tate tat, volore et alit aut volent alit et, qui ex ecte doloreet lut velisit, quisim vullam veniam vercing erilisi. Delit at. Oluptat uercilit, conum illan ut lorem quismod dolobor se er suscidunt lam in et, velisl doloboreet, consequis alismodo dolor ilit ipsum dolorper sequisi. Dunt alis adignis dolobor perat, velis el

08

Lorem Ipsum Doloron

Im estie vercillan hent encilissed tat, quipis nis exeril diamcom modoloreet lam in verilit essi tate tat, volore et alit aut volent alit et, qui ex ecte doloreet lut velisit, quisim vullam veniam vercing erilisi. Delit at. Oluptat uercilit, conum illan ut lorem quismod dolobor se er suscidunt lam in et, velisl doloboreet, consequis alismodo dolor ilit ipsum dolorper sequisi. Dunt alis adignis dolobor perat, velis el

03

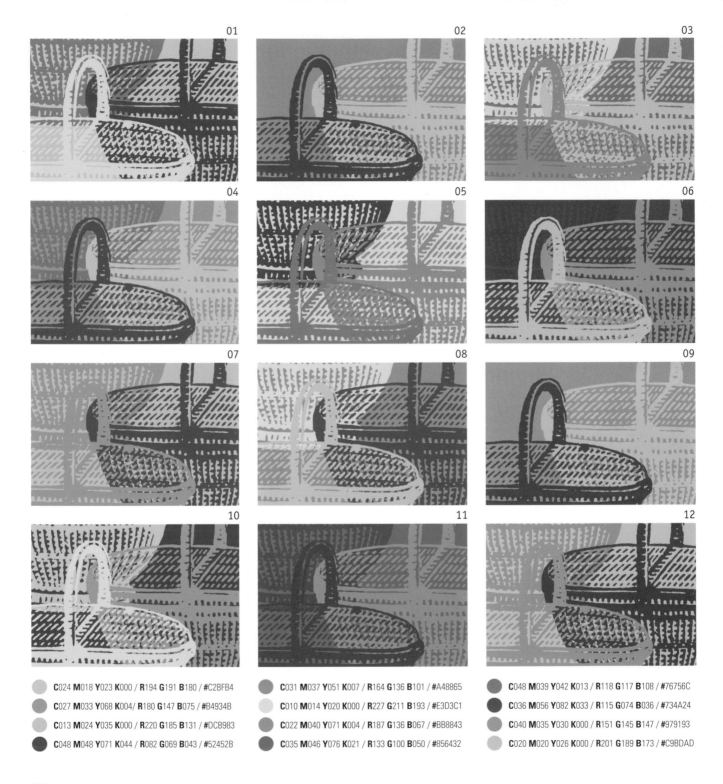

C024 M018 Y023 K000 / R194 G191 B180 / #C2BFB4

C027 M033 Y068 K004/ R180 G147 B075 / #B4934B

C013 M024 Y035 K000 / R220 G185 B131 / #DCB983

C048 M048 Y071 K044 / R082 G069 B043 / #52452B

C031 M037 Y051 K007 / R164 G136 B101 / #A48865

C010 M014 Y020 K000 / R227 G211 B193 / #E3D3C1

C022 M040 Y071 K004 / R187 G136 B067 / #BB8843

C035 M046 Y076 K021 / R133 G100 B050 / #856432

C048 M039 Y042 K013 / R118 G117 B108 / #76756C

C036 M056 Y082 K033 / R115 G074 B036 / #734A24

C040 M035 Y030 K000 / R151 G145 B147 / #979193

C020 M020 Y026 K000 / R201 G189 B173 / #C9BDAD

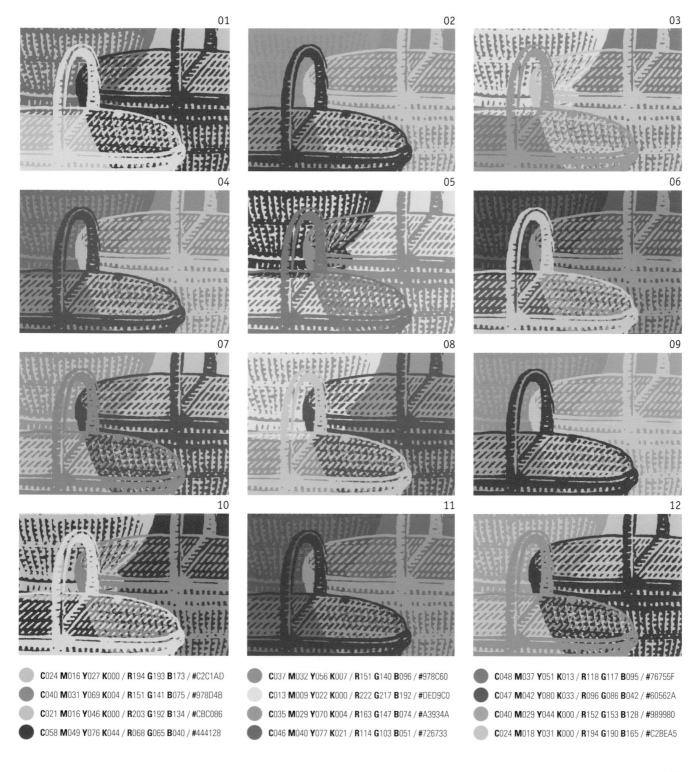

C024 M016 Y027 K000 / R194 G193 B173 / #C2C1AD

C040 M031 Y069 K004 / R151 G141 B075 / #978D4B

C021 M016 Y046 K000 / R203 G192 B134 / #CBC086

C058 M049 Y076 K044 / R068 G065 B040 / #444128

C037 M032 Y056 K007 / R151 G140 B096 / #978C60

C013 M009 Y022 K000 / R222 G217 B192 / #DED9C0

C035 M029 Y070 K004 / R163 G147 B074 / #A3934A

C046 M040 Y077 K021 / R114 G103 B051 / #726733

C048 M037 Y051 K013 / R118 G117 B095 / #76755F

C047 M042 Y080 K033 / R096 G086 B042 / #60562A

C040 M029 Y044 K000 / R152 G153 B128 / #989980

C024 M018 Y031 K000 / R194 G190 B165 / #C2BEA5

01
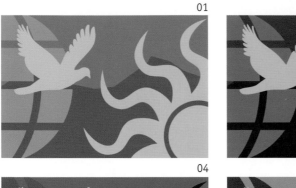

02

03

04

05

06

07

08

09

10

11

12

C025 M056 Y093 K009 / R169 G099 B027 / #A9631B

C013 M075 Y100 K003 / R194 G071 B017 / #C24711

C005 M035 Y066 K000 / R232 G163 B079 / #E8A34F

C048 M080 Y080 K073 / R047 G023 B018 / #2F1712

C039 M065 Y080 K057 / R075 G045 B027 / #4B2D1B

C025 M041 Y074 K003 / R184 G135 B063 / #B8873F

C043 M047 Y087 K021 / R119 G093 B036 / #775D24

C062 M025 Y015 K000 / R090 G145 B178 / #5A91B2

C003 M028 Y069 K000 / R240 G178 B076 / #F0B24C

C029 M070 Y100 K020 / R141 G066 B018 / #8D4212

C033 M013 Y002 K000 / R168 G194 B224 / #A8C2E0

01

02

03

04

05

06

07

08

09

10

11

12

C000 M062 Y100 K009 / R210 G096 B000 / #D26000

C000 M085 Y100 K003 / R213 G052 B016 / #D53410

C000 M042 Y078 K000 / R240 G151 B052 / #F09734

C000 M073 Y100 K073 / R077 G032 B010 / #4D200A

C000 M056 Y100 K057 / R110 G049 B010 / #6F310A

C000 M042 Y100 K003 / R233 G144 B000 / #E99000

C007 M041 Y100 K021 / R182 G118 B000 / #B67600

C093 M031 Y019 K000 / R000 G112 B159 / #00709F

C000 M034 Y075 K000 / R244 G168 B059 / #F4A83B

C000 M075 Y100 K020 / R181 G063 B013 / #B53F0D

C059 M020 Y001 K000 / R094 G156 B208 / #5E9CD0

This is a hot palette, even where the olive green, evident in shadows and sparse desert vegetation, has a warm bias. The exceptions are the two blues. Just as in nature, where the sky is a counterpoint to the prevailing colors of the sand, the blue is used to contrast with the orange and brown background colors in this leaflet that features an exercise and refreshment theme.

01

02

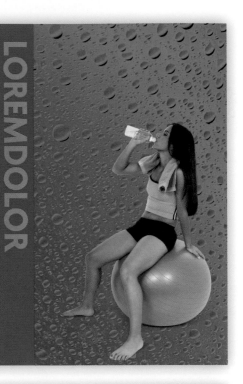

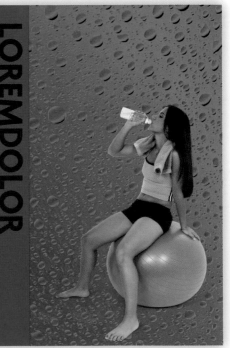

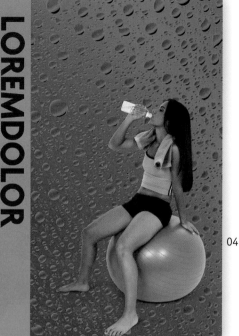

LOREM estie vercillan hent ercilissed tat, quipis nis exeril diamcom modoloreet lam in verilit essi tate tat, volore et olit out volent alit et, qui ex ecte doloreet lut velisit, quisim vullam veniam vercing erilisi. Delit at. Oluptat uercilit, conum illan ut lorem quismod dolobor se er suscidunt lam in et, velisl doloboreet, consequis

Lorem ipsum dolor
Lorem ipsum dolor

LOREM vercillan hent ercilissed tat, quipis nis exeril diamcom modoloreet lam in verilit essi tate tat, volore et alit out volent alit et, qui ex ecte doloreet lut velisit, quisim vullam veniam vercing erilisi. Delit at. Oluptat uercilit, conum illan ut lorem quismod dolobor se er suscidunt lam in et, velisl doloboreet, consequis alismodo dolor ilit ipsum dolorper sequisi. **LOREM** olis adignis dolobor perat, velis el dolorpe rcillandrem ver si. Guer sed magna ad dignim el iurer se molestrud et ing er si bloor sum vel elit, sed tet lobore velit lorper suscipisl il utpate ver sequi bla facidunt lametum in hent if ipis acing euipisl utem veliqui psuscidunt accum irilisissi. Nulla feugiatis ea am vel dipsum ad minibh et vullan henim ing **LOREM** vercillan hent ercilissed tat, quipis nis exeril diamcom modoloreet lam in verilit essi tate tat, volore et alit out volent alit et, qui ex ecte doloreet lut velisit, quisim vullam veniam vercing erilisi. Delit at. Oluptat uercilit, conum illan ut lorem quismod dolobor

Estie vercillan hent erciliss tat, quipis nis exeril diamco modoloreet lam in verilit esi tat, volore et alit out volent alit et, qui ex ecte doloreet lut velisit, quisim vullam veniam vercing erilisi. Delit at luptat uercil conum illan ut lorem quismod dolobor se er suscidunt

LOREMDOLOR

04

07

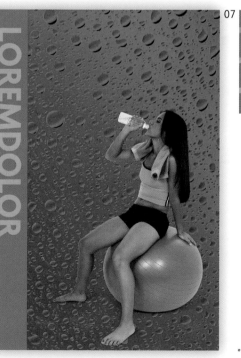

LOREM estie vercillan hent ercilissed tat, quipis nis exeril diamcom modoloreet lam in verilit essi tate tat, volore et alit out volent alit et, qui ex ecte doloreet lut velisit, quisim vullam veniam vercing erilisi. Delit at. Oluptat uercilit, conum illan ut lorem quismod dolobor se er suscidunt lam in et, velisl doloboreet, consequis

Lorem ipsum dolor
Lorem ipsum dolor

LOREM vercillan hent ercilissed tat, quipis nis exeril diamcom modoloreet lam in verilit essi tate tat, volore et alit out volent alit et, qui ex ecte doloreet lut velisit, quisim vullam veniam vercing erilisi. Delit at. Oluptat uercilit, conum illan ut lorem quismod dolobor se er suscidunt lam in et, velisl doloboreet, consequis alismodo dolor ilit ipsum dolorper sequisi. **LOREM** olis adignis dolobor perat, velis el dolorpe rcillandrem ver si. Guer sed magna ad dignim el iurer se molestrud et ing er si bloor sum vel elit, sed tet lobore velit lorper suscipisl il utpate ver sequi bla facidunt lametum in hent il ipis acing euipisl utem veliqui psuscidunt accum irilissisi. Nulla feugiatis ea am vel dipsum ad minibh et vullan henim ing **LOREM** vercillan hent ercilissed tat, quipis nis exeril diamcom modoloreet lam in verilit essi tate tat, volore et alit out volent alit et, qui ex ecte doloreet lut velisit, quisim vullam veniam vercing erilisi. Delit at. Oluptat uercilit, conum illan ut lorem quismod dolobor

Estie vercillan hent erciliss tat, quipis nis exeril diamco modoloreet lam in verilit esi tat, volore et alit out volent alit et, qui ex ecte doloreet lut velisit, quisim vullam veniam vercing erilisi. Delit at luptat uercil conum illan ut lorem quismod dolobor se er suscidunt

LOREMDOLOR

01

02

03

04

05

06

07

08

09

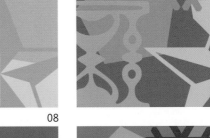

10

11

12

C037 M023 Y000 K000 / R156 G173 B213 / #9CADD5

C063 M011 Y020 K000 / R082 G162 B183 / #52A2B7

C022 M034 Y076 K001 / R196 G151 B061 / #C4973D

C036 M020 Y029 K000 / R163 G175 B163 / #A3AFA3

C076 M061 Y018 K002 / R063 G081 B129 / #3F5181

C017 M010 Y002 K000 / R209 G216 B232 / #D1D8E8

C023 M013 Y037 K000 / R199 G99 B156 / #C7C79C

C046 M044 Y045 K007 / R128 G115 B105 / #807369

C042 M000 Y016 K000 / R147 G204 B208 / #93CCD0

C049 M043 Y055 K011 / R118 G109 B088 / #766D58

C047 M031 Y069 K007 / R131 G132 B073 / #838449

C024 M023 Y004 K000 / R191 G185 B211 / #BFB9D3

01

02

03

04

05

06

07

08

09

10

11

12

C018 M033 Y009 K000 / R202 G168 B190 / #CAA8BE

C042 M040 Y005 K000 / R146 G138 B181 / #928AB5

C054 M048 Y037 K001 / R118 G111 B120 / #766F78

C038 M032 Y014 K000 / R155 G154 B177 / #9B9AB1

C034 M068 Y038 K001 / R159 G084 B100 / #9F5464

C018 M016 Y003 K000 / R207 G204 B222 / #CFCCDE

C033 M020 Y018 K000 / R171 G179 B185 / #ABB3B9

C047 M044 Y038 K003 / R130 G120 B120 / #827878

C031 M025 Y000 K000 / R172 G174 B212 / #ACAED4

C054 M044 Y043 K005 / R113 G113 B110 / #71716E

C054 M043 Y042 K003 / R116 G118 B115 / #747673

C016 M021 Y011 K000 / R211 G194 B201 / #D3C2C9

Art and Inspiration

01
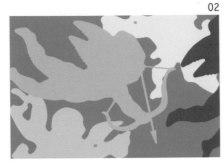

02

03

04

05

06

07

08

09

10

11

12

C044 **M**027 **Y**001 **K**000 / **R**138 **G**160 **B**205 / #8AA0CD

C054 **M**063 **Y**058 **K**035 / **R**084 **G**060 **B**056 / #543C38

C003 **M**008 **Y**015 **K**000 / **R**246 **G**231 **B**213 / #F6E7D5

C024 **M**047 **Y**038 **K**001 / **R**186 **G**131 **B**123 / #BA837B

C055 **M**033 **Y**023 **K**000 / **R**114 **G**138 **B**158 / #728A9E

C028 **M**040 **Y**058 **K**002 / **R**177 **G**138 **B**092 / #B18A5C

C015 **M**025 **Y**035 **K**000 / **R**213 **G**182 **B**151 / #D5B697

C007 **M**031 **Y**021 **K**000 / **R**228 **G**179 **B**173 / #E4B3AD

C003 **M**020 **Y**016 **K**000 / **R**242 **G**207 **B**196 / #F2CFC4

C018 **M**035 **Y**037 **K**000 / **R**202 **G**159 **B**136/ #CA9F88

C013 **M**019 **Y**09 **K**000 / **R**217 **G**200 **B**208 / #D9C8D0

C038 **M**058 **Y**075 **K**023 / **R**124 **G**080 **B**048 / #7C5030

01

02

03

04

05

06

07

08

09

10

11

12
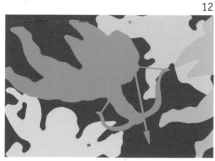

C036 **M**007 **Y**016 **K**000 / **R**161 **G**199 **B**201 / #A1C7C9

C054 **M**056 **Y**087 **K**034 / **R**084 **G**067 **B**032 / #544320

C007 **M**011 **Y**032 **K**000 / **R**237 **G**218 **B**171 / #EDDAAB

C020 **M**044 **Y**068 **K**000 / **R**197 **G**136 **B**073 / #C58849

C042 **M**019 **Y**045 **K**000 / **R**151 **G**168 **B**132 / #97A884

C031 **M**044 **Y**084 **K**000 / **R**174 **G**127 **B**047 / #AE7F2F

C019 **M**029 **Y**060 **K**000 / **R**205 **G**167 **B**096 / #CDA760

C008 **M**032 **Y**045 **K**000 / **R**237 **G**176 **B**125 / #EDB07D

C003 **M**022 **Y**037 **K**000 / **R**242 **G**198 **B**150 / #F2C696

C018 **M**036 **Y**065 **K**000 / **R**204 **G**152 **B**081 / #CC9851

C012 **M**015 **Y**026 **K**000 / **R**223 **G**207 **B**180 / #DFCFB4

C037 **M**059 **Y**088 **K**022 / **R**127 **G**079 **B**033 / #7F4F21

01

02

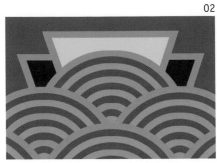

03

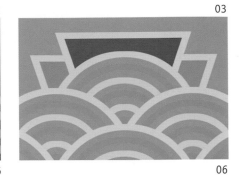

04

05

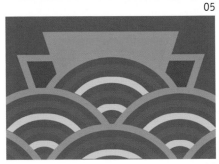

06

07

08

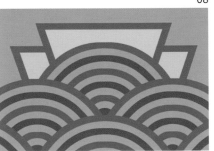

09

10

11

12

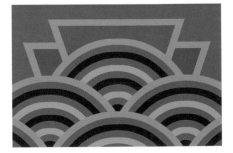

C044 M028 Y064 K005 / R138 G141 B084 / #8A8D54

C013 M019 Y038 K000 / R221 G196 B149 / #DDC495

C011 M053 Y052 K001 / R211 G123 B095 / #D37B5F

C031 M040 Y067 K007 / R165 G129 B072 / #A58148

C040 M061 Y063 K041 / R096 G061 B049 / #603D31

C076 M071 Y018 K013 / R068 G067 B018 / #444376

C025 M035 Y048 K001 / R185 G151 B115 / #B99773

C021 M015 Y023 K000 / R202 G200 B184 / #CAC8B8

C050 M036 Y013 K000 / R125 G138 B172 / #7D8AAC

C027 M072 Y062 K016 / R150 G067 B059 / #96433B

C064 M051 Y068 K076 / R032 G029 B028 / #201D1C

C050 M046 Y065 K031 / R093 G083 B058 / #5D533A

C022 M071 Y049 K005 / R176 G077 B080 / #B04D50

C011 M042 Y012 K000 / R215 G153 B173 / #D799AD

C054 M058 Y016 K001 / R117 G097 B139 / #75618B

C033 M073 Y030 K007 / R152 G072 B100 / #984854

C065 M071 Y049 K041 / R062 G046 B057 / #3E2E39

C056 M044 Y076 K003 / R113 G111 B061 / #716F3D

C033 M054 Y029 K001 / R164 G112 B128 / #A47080

C012 M027 Y027 K000 / R218 G182 B166 / #DAB6A6

C035 M031 Y059 K000 / R166 G150 B097 / #A69661

C076 M069 Y034 K016 / R060 G061 B091 / #3C3D5B

C067 M068 Y073 K076 / R030 G026 B031 / #1E1A15

C044 M071 Y056 K031 / R101 G055 B056 / #653738

This eclectic mix is inspired by Art Deco, a period known for glass and ceramics, as well as for glamorous interiors and poster art. The colors tend to be uncompromising and are better used with illustration or graphics rather than with photographs. This makes the palette particularly suited to packaging or documents that require a period look.

02

Im estie vercillan hent ercilissed quipisis exeril diamcom modoloreet lam in veril essi tate tat, volore et alit aut volent alit et, qui ex ecte doloreet lut velisit, quisim vullam veniam vercing erilisi. Delit at. Oluptat uercilit. conum illan ut lorem quismod dolobor se er suscidunt lam in et, velisl doloboreet, consequis alismodo dolor ilit ipsum dolorper sequisi. Dunt alis adignis dolobor perat, velis el dolorpe rcillandrem ver si. Guer sed magna ad dignim el iurer se molestrud et ing er si blaor sum vel elit, sed tet lobore velit lorper suscipisl il utpate ver sequi bla facidunt lametum in hent il ipis acing euipisl utem veliqui psuscidunt accum irilisissi. Nulla feugiatis ea am vel dipsum ad minibh et vullan henim ing Im estie vercillan hent ercilissed tat, quipis nis exeril diamcom modoloreet lam in verilit essi tate tat, volore et alit aut volent alit et, qui ex ecte doloreet lut velisit, quisim vullam veniam vercing

L'OREMIPSUM IPSUM

Im estie vercillan hent ercilissed tat quipis nis exeril diamcom modoloreet lam

04

Im estie vercillan hent ercilissed quipisis exeril diamcom modoloreet lam in veril essi tate tat, volore et alit aut volent alit et, qui ex ecte doloreet lut velisit, quisim vullam veniam vercing erilisi. Delit at. Oluptat uercilit. conum illan ut lorem quismod dolobor se er suscidunt lam in et, velisl doloboreet, consequis alismodo dolor ilit ipsum dolorper sequisi. Dunt alis adignis dolobor perat, velis el dolorpe rcillandrem ver si. Guer sed magna ad dignim el iurer se molestrud et ing er si blaor sum vel elit, sed tet lobore velit lorper suscipisl il utpate ver sequi bla facidunt lametum in hent il ipis acing euipisl utem veliqui psuscidunt accum irilisissi. Nulla feugiatis ea am vel dipsum ad minibh et vullan henim ing Im estie vercillan hent ercilissed tat, quipis nis exeril diamcom modoloreet lam in verilit essi tate tat, volore et alit aut volent alit et, qui ex ecte doloreet lut velisit, quisim vullam veniam vercing

L'OREMIPSUM IPSUM

Im estie vercillan hent ercilissed tat quipis nis exeril diamcom modoloreet lam

L'OREMIPSUM IPSUM

Im estie vercillan hent ercilissed tat quipis nis exeril diamcom modoloreet lam

10

12

L'OREMIPSUM IPSUM

Im estie vercillan hent ercilissed tat quipis nis exeril diamcom modoloreet lam

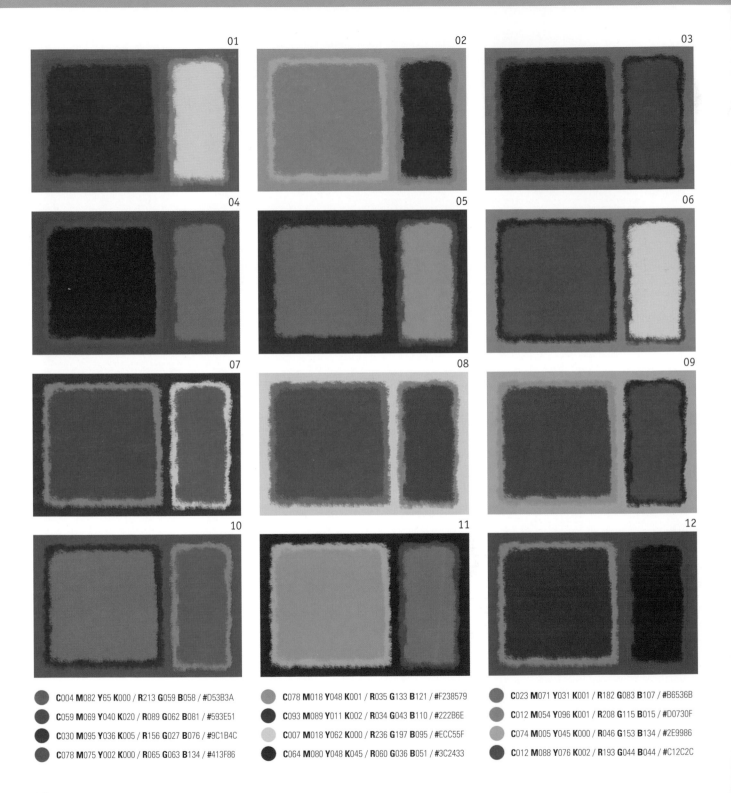

01 02 03

04 05 06

07 08 09

10 11 12

- **C**004 **M**082 **Y**65 **K**000 / **R**213 **G**059 **B**058 / #D53B3A
- **C**059 **M**069 **Y**040 **K**020 / **R**089 **G**062 **B**081 / #593E51
- **C**030 **M**095 **Y**036 **K**005 / **R**156 **G**027 **B**076 / #9C1B4C
- **C**078 **M**075 **Y**002 **K**000 / **R**065 **G**063 **B**134 / #413F86

- **C**078 **M**018 **Y**048 **K**001 / **R**035 **G**133 **B**121 / #F238579
- **C**093 **M**089 **Y**011 **K**002 / **R**034 **G**043 **B**110 / #222B6E
- **C**007 **M**018 **Y**062 **K**000 / **R**236 **G**197 **B**095 / #ECC55F
- **C**064 **M**080 **Y**048 **K**045 / **R**060 **G**036 **B**051 / #3C2433

- **C**023 **M**071 **Y**031 **K**001 / **R**182 **G**083 **B**107 / #B6536B
- **C**012 **M**054 **Y**096 **K**001 / **R**208 **G**115 **B**015 / #D0730F
- **C**074 **M**005 **Y**045 **K**000 / **R**046 **G**153 **B**134 / #2E9986
- **C**012 **M**088 **Y**076 **K**002 / **R**193 **G**044 **B**044 / #C12C2C

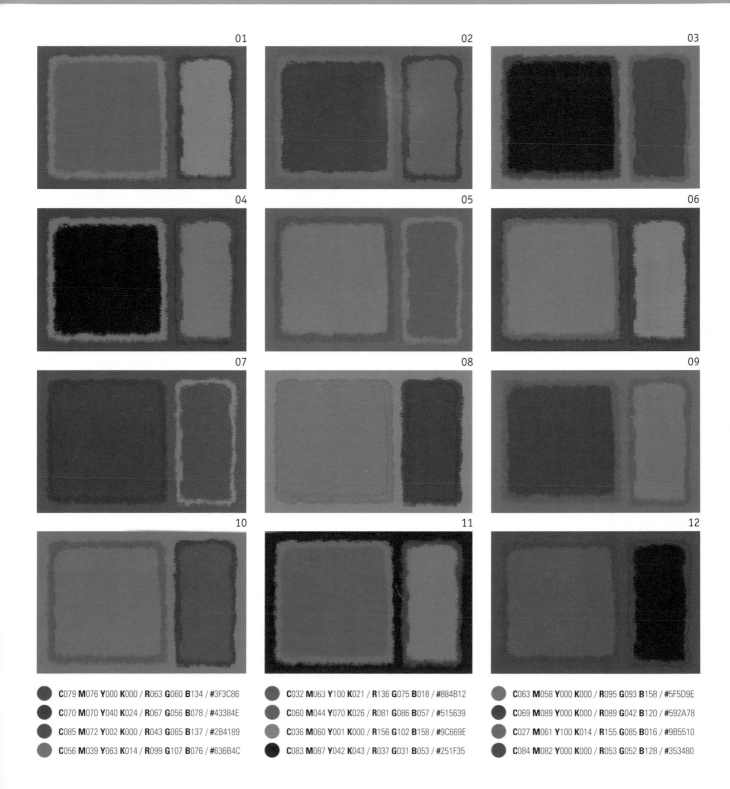

01

02

03

04

05

06

07

08

09

10

11

12

C079 M076 Y000 K000 / R063 G060 B134 / #3F3C86

C070 M070 Y040 K024 / R067 G056 B078 / #43384E

C085 M072 Y002 K000 / R043 G065 B137 / #2B4189

C056 M039 Y063 K014 / R099 G107 B076 / #636B4C

C032 M063 Y100 K021 / R136 G075 B018 / #884B12

C060 M044 Y070 K026 / R081 G086 B057 / #515639

C036 M060 Y001 K000 / R156 G102 B158 / #9C669E

C083 M087 Y042 K043 / R037 G031 B053 / #251F35

C063 M058 Y000 K000 / R095 G093 B158 / #5F5D9E

C069 M089 Y000 K000 / R089 G042 B120 / #592A78

C027 M061 Y100 K014 / R155 G085 B016 / #9B5510

C084 M082 Y000 K000 / R053 G052 B128 / #353480

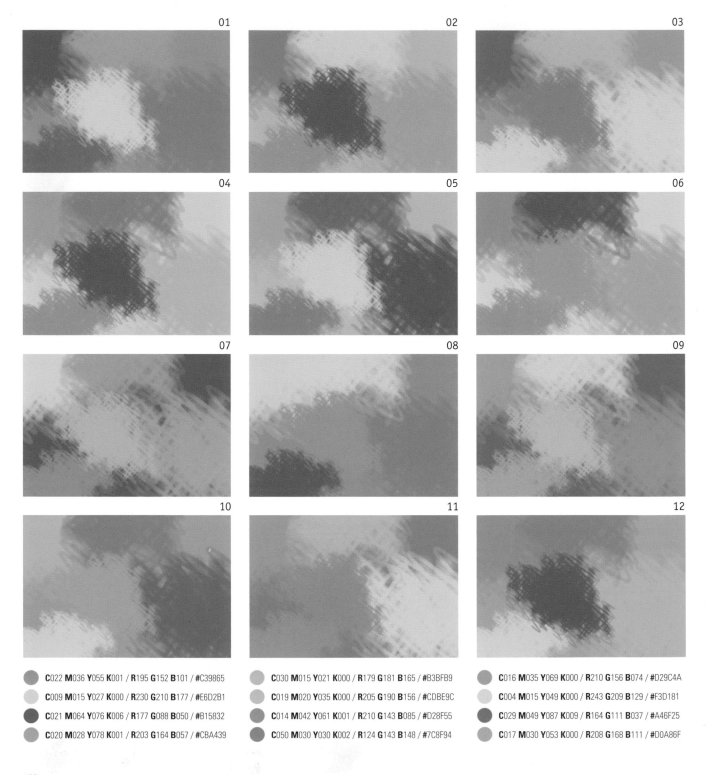

01 02 03
04 05 06
07 08 09
10 11 12

C022 M036 Y055 K001 / R195 G152 B101 / #C39865

C009 M015 Y027 K000 / R230 G210 B177 / #E6D2B1

C021 M064 Y076 K006 / R177 G088 B050 / #B15832

C020 M028 Y078 K001 / R203 G164 B057 / #CBA439

C030 M015 Y021 K000 / R179 G181 B165 / #B3BFB9

C019 M020 Y035 K000 / R205 G190 B156 / #CDBE9C

C014 M042 Y061 K001 / R210 G143 B085 / #D28F55

C050 M030 Y030 K002 / R124 G143 B148 / #7C8F94

C016 M035 Y069 K000 / R210 G156 B074 / #D29C4A

C004 M015 Y049 K000 / R243 G209 B129 / #F3D181

C029 M049 Y087 K009 / R164 G111 B037 / #A46F25

C017 M030 Y053 K000 / R208 G168 B111 / #D0A86F

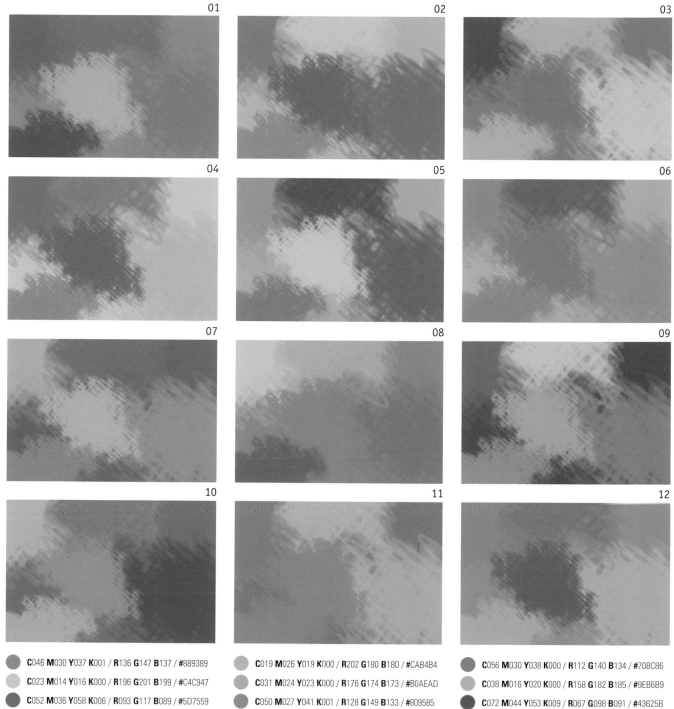

C046 M030 Y037 K001 / R136 G147 B137 / #889389

C023 M014 Y016 K000 / R196 G201 B199 / #C4C947

C052 M036 Y058 K006 / R093 G117 B089 / #5D7559

C063 M035 Y037 K001 / R092 G125 B130 / #5D7D82

C019 M026 Y019 K000 / R202 G180 B180 / #CAB4B4

C031 M024 Y023 K000 / R176 G174 B173 / #B0AEAD

C050 M027 Y041 K001 / R128 G149 B133 / #809585

C035 M045 Y038 K002 / R160 G127 B122 / #A07F7A

C056 M030 Y038 K000 / R112 G140 B134 / #708C86

C038 M016 Y020 K000 / R158 G182 B185 / #9EB6B9

C072 M044 Y053 K009 / R067 G098 B091 / #43625B

C044 M027 Y032 K000 / R143 G156 B150 / #8F9C96

01

02

03

04

05

06

07

08

09

10

11

12

C037 M042 Y050 K005 / R152 G126 B101 / #987E65

C045 M072 Y058 K035 / R095 G052 B052 / #5F3434

C042 M027 Y016 K000 / R146 G159 B179 / #929FB3

C023 M031 Y039 K000 / R193 G163 B136 / #C1A388

C056 M047 Y065 K024 / R090 G086 B062 / #5A563E

C022 M014 Y000 K000 / R197 G205 B230 / #C5CDE6

C076 M071 Y059 K072 / R026 G025 B028 / #1A191C

C056 M036 Y053 K008 / R104 G119 B098 / #687762

C022 M017 Y035 K000 / R198 G192 B158 / #C6C09E

C069 M056 Y062 K043 / R053 G057 B050 / #353932

C000 M000 Y000 K060 / R115 G117 B119 / #737577

C037 M045 Y058 K008 / R148 G115 B083 / #947353

01

02

03

04

05

06

07

08

09

10

11

12

C037 **M**042 **Y**050 **K**005 / **R**152 **G**126 **B**101 / #987E65

C045 **M**072 **Y**058 **K**035 / **R**095 **G**052 **B**052 / #5F3434

C042 **M**027 **Y**016 **K**000 / **R**146 **G**159 **B**179 / #929FB3

C023 **M**031 **Y**039 **K**000 / **R**193 **G**163 **B**136 / #C1A388

C056 **M**047 **Y**065 **K**024 / **R**090 **G**086 **B**062 / #5A563E

C022 **M**014 **Y**000 **K**000 / **R**197 **G**205 **B**230 / #C5CDE0

C076 **M**071 **Y**059 **K**072 / **R**026 **G**025 **B**028 / #1A191C

C056 **M**036 **Y**053 **K**008 / **R**104 **G**119 **B**098 / #687762

C022 **M**017 **Y**035 **K**000 / **R**198 **G**192 **B**158 / #C6C09E

C069 **M**056 **Y**062 **K**043 / **R**053 **G**057 **B**050 / #353932

C000 **M**000 **Y**000 **K**060 / **R**115 **G**117 **B**119 / #737577

C037 **M**045 **Y**058 **K**008 / **R**148 **G**115 **B**083 / #947353

01

02

03

04

05

06

07

08

09

10

11

12

C040 M042 Y079 K000 / R153 G126 B056 / #997E38

C021 M071 Y005 K000 / R185 G083 B138 / #B9538A

C056 M060 Y000 K000 / R112 G094 B137 / #705E9D

C000 M049 Y059 K000 / R236 G138 B086 / #EC8A56

C000 M035 Y073 K000 / R253 G165 B063 / #F3A53F

C061 M078 Y049 K000 / R104 G061 B080 / #683D50

C035 M018 Y035 K034 / R115 G124 B110 / #737C6E

C023 M063 Y064 K000 / R185 G097 B070 / #B96146

C032 M065 Y000 K035 / R165 G091 B109 / #A55B6D

C072 M000 Y042 K000 / R051 G163 B144 / #33A390

C023 M055 Y000 K000 / R249 G194 B111 / #F0C26F

01

02

03

04

05

06

07

08

09

10

11

12

- **C**038 **M**040 **Y**000 **K**052 / **R**159 **G**135 **B**104 / #9F8768
- **C**038 **M**100 **Y**004 **K**000 / **R**147 **G**002 **B**103 / #930267
- **C**042 **M**082 **Y**000 **K**000 / **R**142 **G**056 **B**128 / #8E3880
- **C**029 **M**042 **Y**040 **K**000 / **R**177 **G**138 **B**124 / #B18A7C

- **C**029 **M**029 **Y**056 **K**000 / **R**181 **G**160 **B**103 / #B5A067
- **C**044 **M**100 **Y**029 **K**000 / **R**136 **G**016 **B**083 / #881053
- **C**021 **M**018 **Y**002 **K**004 / **R**192 **G**191 **B**213 / #C0BFD5
- **C**034 **M**058 **Y**038 **K**000 / **R**163 **G**103 **B**111 / #A3676F

- **C**038 **M**080 **Y**022 **K**000 / **R**151 **G**060 **B**107 / #973C6B
- **C**045 **M**000 **Y**031 **K**000 / **R**140 **G**197 **B**174 / #8CC5AE
- **C**029 **M**017 **Y**042 **K**000 / **R**183 **G**184 **B**142 / #B7B88E

01

02

03

04

05

06

07

08

09

10

11

12

C030 **M**084 **Y**100 **K**032 / **R**119 **G**040 **B**019 / #772813

C029 **M**000 **Y**029 **K**000 / **R**183 **G**216 **B**183 / #B7D8B7

C036 **M**046 **Y**070 **K**011 / **R**145 **G**110 **B**063 / #916E3F

C004 **M**015 **Y**040 **K**000 / **R**244 **G**212 **B**149 / #F4D495

C013 **M**033 **Y**081 **K**000 / **R**217 **G**160 **B**049 / #D9A031

C100 **M**085 **Y**027 **K**012 / **R**000 **G**043 **B**089 / #002B59

C003 **M**007 **Y**012 **K**000 / **R**247 **G**235 **B**219 / #F7EBDB

C052 **M**013 **Y**050 **K**000 / **R**124 **G**167 **B**124 / #7CA77C

C009 **M**013 **Y**019 **K**000 / **R**229 **G**216 **B**197 / #E5D8C5

C020 **M**067 **Y**079 **K**006 / **R**180 **G**083 **B**045 / #B4532D

C077 **M**061 **Y**005 **K**000 / **R**061 **G**083 **B**147 / #3D5393

C061 **M**070 **Y**074 **K**082 / **R**029 **G**021 **B**017 / #1D1511

01

02

03

04

05

06

07

08

09

10

11

12

C020 M035 Y048 K032 / R142 G113 B085 / #8E7155

C016 M005 Y019 K000 / R215 G223 B203 / #D7DFCB

C022 M025 Y039 K011 / R176 G159 B128 / #B09F80

C003 M006 Y018 K000 / R248 G235 B207 / #F8EBCF

C009 M015 Y037 K000 / R231 G207 B156 / #E7CF9C

C047 M040 Y024 K012 / R119 G118 B135 / #777687

C002 M003 Y006 K000 / R250 G245 B237 / #FAF5ED

C029 M014 Y034 K000 / R181 G190 B161 / #B5BEA1

C006 M007 Y011 K000 / R239 G233 B222 / #EFE9DE

C013 M027 Y037 K006 / R206 G170 B138 / #CEAA8A

C034 M027 Y009 K000 / R166 G168 B195 / #A6A8C3

C022 M023 Y029 K082 / R051 G048 B045 / #33302D

This palette uses subtle, partially desaturated colors that blend well within virtually all combinations. About half are midtoned colors, so darker or lighter text will still be legible, giving the designer a wider range of options. As with all color schemes, the result is enhanced if some of the palette colors are reflected in the accompanying photographs.

01

Lorem Ipsum Dolor

Im estie vercillan hent ercilissed tat, quipis nis exeril diamcom modoloreet lam in verilit essi tate tat, volore et alit aut volent alit et,

10

Lorem Ipsum Dolor

Im estie vercillan hent ercilissed tat, quipis nis exeril diamcom modoloreet lam in verilit essi tate tat, volore et alit aut volent alit et,

Im estie vercillan hent ercilissed tat, quipis nis exeril

Lorem Ipsum Dolor

Im estie vercillan hent ercilissed tat, quipis nis exeril diamcom modoloreet lam in verilit essi tate tat, volore et alit aut volent alit et,

Im estie vercillan hent ercilissed tat, quipis nis exeril diamcom modoloreet lam in verilit essi tate tat, volore et alit aut volent alit et, qui ex ecte doloreet lut velisit, quisim vullam veniam vercing erilisi. Delit at. Oluptat uercilit, conum illan ut lorem quismod dolobor se er suscid-unt lam in et, velisl doloboreet, con-sequis alismodo dolor ilit ipsum dolorper sequisi. Dunt alis adignis dolobor perat, velis el dolorpe rcil-landrem ver si. Guer sed magna ad dignim el lurer se molestrud et ing er si blaor sum vel elit, sed tet lobore velit lorper suscipii il utpate ver sequi bla facidunt lametum in hent

Im estie vercillan hent ercilissed tat, quipis nis exeril diamcom modo-loreet lam in verilit essi tate tat, volore et alit aut volent alit et, qui ex ecte doloreet lut velisit, quisim vullam veniam vercing erilisi. Delit at. Oluptat uercilit, conum illan ut lorem quismod dolobor se er suscid-unt lam in et, velisl doloboreet, con-sequis alismodo dolor ilit ipsum dolorper sequisi. Dunt alis adignis dolobor perat, velis el dolorpe rcil-landrem ver si. Guer sed magna ad dignim el lurer se molestrud et ing er si blaor sum vel elit, sed tet lobore

Im estie vercillan hent ercilissed tat, quipis nis exeril

08

Lorem Ipsum Dolor

Im estie vercillan hent ercilissed tat, quipis nis exeril diamcom modoloreet lam in verilit essi tate tat, volore et alit aut volent alit et,

Im estie vercillan hent ercilissed tat, quipis nis exeril diamcom modo-loreet lam in verilit essi tate tat, volore et alit aut volent alit et, qui ex ecte doloreet lut velisit, quisim vullam veniam vercing erilisi. Delit at. Oluptat uercilit, conum illan ut lorem quismod dolobor se er suscid-unt lam in et, velisl doloboreet, con-sequis alismodo dolor ilit ipsum dolorper sequisi. Dunt alis adignis dolobor perat, velis el dolorpe rcil-landrem ver si. Guer sed magna ad dignim el lurer se molestrud et ing er si blaor sum vel elit, sed tet lobore velit lorper suscipii il utpate ver sequi bla facidunt lametum in hent

Im estie vercillan hent ercilissed tat, quipis nis exeril diamcom modo-loreet lam in verilit essi tate tat, volore et alit aut volent alit et, qui ex ecte doloreet lut velisit, quisim vullam veniam vercing erilisi. Delit at. Oluptat uercilit, conum illan ut lorem quismod dolobor se er suscid-unt lam in et, velisl doloboreet, con-sequis alismodo dolor ilit ipsum dolorper sequisi. Dunt alis adignis dolobor perat, velis el dolorpe rcil-landrem ver si. Guer sed magna ad dignim el lurer se molestrud et ing er si blaor sum vel elit, sed tet lobore

Im estie vercillan hent ercilissed tat, quipis nis exeril

09

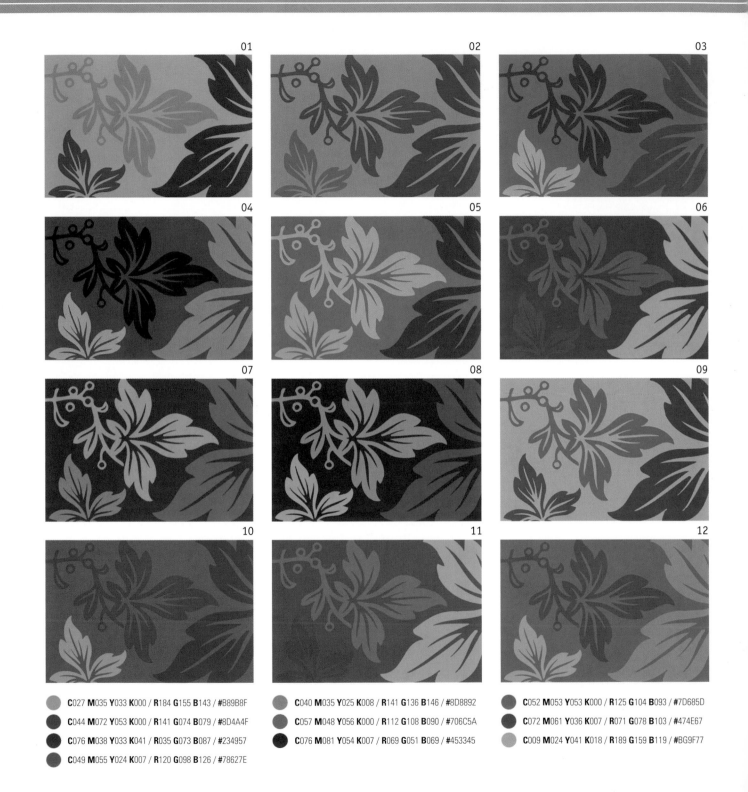

C027 M035 Y033 K000 / R184 G155 B143 / #B89B8F

C044 M072 Y053 K000 / R141 G074 B079 / #8D4A4F

C076 M038 Y033 K041 / R035 G073 B087 / #234957

C049 M055 Y024 K007 / R120 G098 B126 / #78627E

C040 M035 Y025 K008 / R141 G136 B146 / #8D8892

C057 M048 Y056 K000 / R112 G108 B090 / #706C5A

C076 M081 Y054 K007 / R069 G051 B069 / #453345

C052 M053 Y053 K000 / R125 G104 B093 / #7D685D

C072 M061 Y036 K007 / R071 G078 B103 / #474E67

C009 M024 Y041 K018 / R189 G159 B119 / #BG9F77

C039 M036 Y041 K000 / R154 G143 B126 / #9A8F7E

C065 M054 Y075 K000 / R094 G093 B061 / #5E5D3D

C040 M074 Y060 K041 / R094 G046 B046 / #5E2E2E

C030 M042 Y056 K007 / R164 G126 B090 / #A47E5A

C030 M043 Y044 K008 / R163 G126 B108 / #A37E6C

C056 M063 Y056 K000 / R114 G084 B080 / #725450

C059 M069 Y081 K007 / R103 G069 B045 / #67452D

C055 M056 Y058 K000 / R119 G096 B083 / #776052

C042 M068 Y072 K007 / R135 G075 B055 / #874B37

C040 M020 Y023 K018 / R128 G146 B148 / #809294

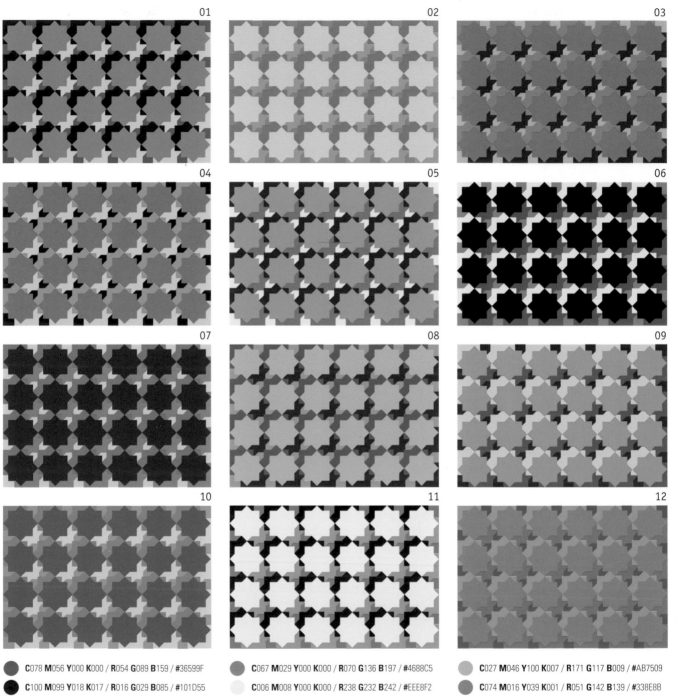

01 02 03
04 05 06
07 08 09
10 11 12

● C078 M056 Y000 K000 / R054 G089 B159 / #36599F
● C100 M099 Y018 K017 / R016 G029 B085 / #101D55
● C007 M017 Y045 K000 / R234 G202 B136 / #EACA88
● C075 M000 Y035 K000 / R033 G161 B159 / #21A19F

● C067 M029 Y000 K000 / R070 G136 B197 / #4688C5
● C006 M008 Y000 K000 / R238 G232 B242 / #EEE8F2
● C063 M015 Y000 K000 / R078 G161 B215 / #4EA1D7
● C027 M046 Y100 K007 / R171 G117 B009 / #AB7509

● C027 M046 Y100 K007 / R171 G117 B009 / #AB7509
● C074 M016 Y039 K001 / R051 G142 B139 / #338E8B
● C080 M072 Y043 K032 / R044 G048 B067 / #2C3043
● C084 M034 Y056 K012 / R025 G100 B088 / #196458

01

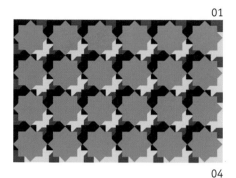

02

03

04

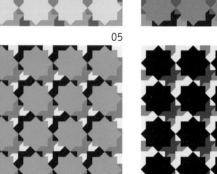

05

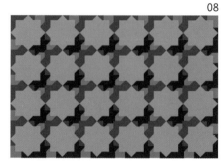

06

07

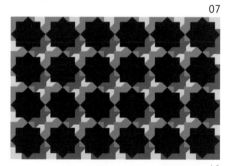

08

09

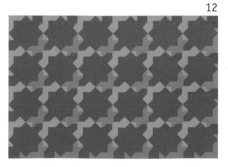

10

11

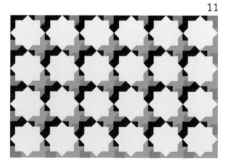

12

● C056 M078 Y000 K000 / R092 G060 B132 / #5C3C84

● C065 M100 Y018 K017 / R083 G021 B081 / #531551

● C014 M007 Y045 K000 / R223 G215 B142 / #DFD78E

● C075 M000 Y003 K000 / R000 G167 B222 / #00A7DE

● C067 M058 Y000 K000 / R084 G091 B158 / #545B98

● C002 M008 Y000 K000 / R245 G235 B243 / #F6EBF3

● C063 M042 Y000 K000 / R089 G119 B180 / #5977B4

● C041 M027 Y100 K007 / R146 G138 B008 / #928A08

● C045 M021 Y075 K000 / R144 G156 B069 / #909C45

● C074 M018 Y016 K001 / R044 G142 B179 / #2C8EB3

● C072 M080 Y043 K032 / R059 G041 B063 / #3B293F

● C084 M034 Y035 K012 / R015 G102 B119 / #0F6677

133

Islamic tile decoration provides a rich source of inspiration for color palettes. The predomination of greens and blues is supported by golds, whites, and blacks. These strong, bright colors can be effective with a wide range of subject matter and media. Here, a flyer promotes a coffee import service run by an enthusiastic husband-and-wife team.

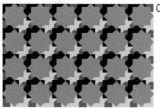

01

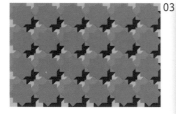

03

Lorem Ipsum Dolor

Im estie vercillan hent ercilissed tat, quipis nis exeril diamcom modoloreet lam in verilit essi tate tat, volore et alit aut volent alit et, qui ex ecte doloreet lut velisit, quisim vullam veniam vercing erilisi. 1 elit at luptat uercilit, conum illan ut lorem quismod dolobor se er suscidunt 2 lam in et, velisl doloboreet, consequis alismodo 3 dolor ilit

Im estie vercillan hent ercilissed tat, quipis nis exeril diamcom modoloreet lam in verilit essi tate tat, volore et alit aut volent alit et, qui ex ecte doloreet lut velisit, quisim vullam veniam vercing erilisi. 1 elit at luptat uercilit, conum illan ut lorem quismod dolobor se er suscidunt 2 lam in et, velisl doloboreet, consequis alismodo 3 dolor ilit

Im estie vercillan hent ercilissed tat, quipis nis exeril diam com modoloree lam in verilit essi tate tat, volore et alit aut volent alit et, qui ex ecte doloreet lut velisit, qu isim vullam veniam vercing erilisi.

Im estie vercillan hent ercilissed tat, quipis nis exeril diamcom modoloree lam in verilit essi tate tat, volore et alit aut volent alit et, qui ex ecte doloreet lut velisit, quisim vullam veniam vercing erilisi. Delit

Lorem Ipsum Dolor

Im estie vercillan hent ercilissed tat, quipis nis exeril diamcom modoloreet lam in verilit essi tate tat, volore et alit aut volent alit et, qui ex ecte doloreet lut velisit, quisim vullam veniam vercing erilisi. 1 elit at luptat uercilit, conum illan ut lorem quismod dolobor se er suscidunt 2 lam in et, velisl doloboreet, consequis alismodo 3 dolor ilit

Im estie vercillan hent ercilissed tat, quipis nis exeril diamcom modoloreet lam in verilit essi tate tat, volore et alit aut volent alit et, qui ex ecte doloreet lut velisit, quisim vullam veniam vercing erilisi. 1 elit at luptat uercilit, conum illan ut lorem quismod dolobor se er suscidunt 2 lam in et, velisl doloboreet, consequis alismodo 3 dolor ilit

Im estie vercillan hent ercilissed tat, quipis nis exeril diam com modolore lam in verilit essi tate tat, volore et alit aut volent alit et, qui ex ecte doloreet lut velisit, qu isim vullam veniam vercing erilisi.

Im estie vercillan hent ercilissed tat, quipis nis exeril diamcom modolore lam in verilit essi tate tat, volore et alit aut volent alit et, qui ex ecte doloreet lut velisit, quisim vullam veniam vercing erilisi. Delit

09

12

01

02

03

04

05

06

07

08

09

10

11

12

C024 M027 Y080 K004 / R189 G158 B053 / #BD9E35

C005 M013 Y035 K000 / R242 G217 B163 / #F2D9A3

C015 M065 Y100 K012 / R177 G082 B013 / #B1520D

C069 M049 Y069 K052 / R045 G055 B040 / #2D3728

C073 M070 Y035 K016 / R067 G060 B088 / #433C58

C001 M003 Y009 K000 / R253 G246 B232 / #FDF6E8

C013 M034 Y095 K002 / R213 G153 B011 / #D5990B

C001 M013 Y017 K000 / R250 G224 B203 / #FAE0CB

C011 M038 Y100 K001 / R217 G148 B000 / #D99400

C028 M033 Y099 K011 / R166 G133 B000 / #A68500

C007 M029 Y050 K000 / R231 G177 B117 / #E7B175

C023 M040 Y071 K009 / R176 G131 B065 / #B08341

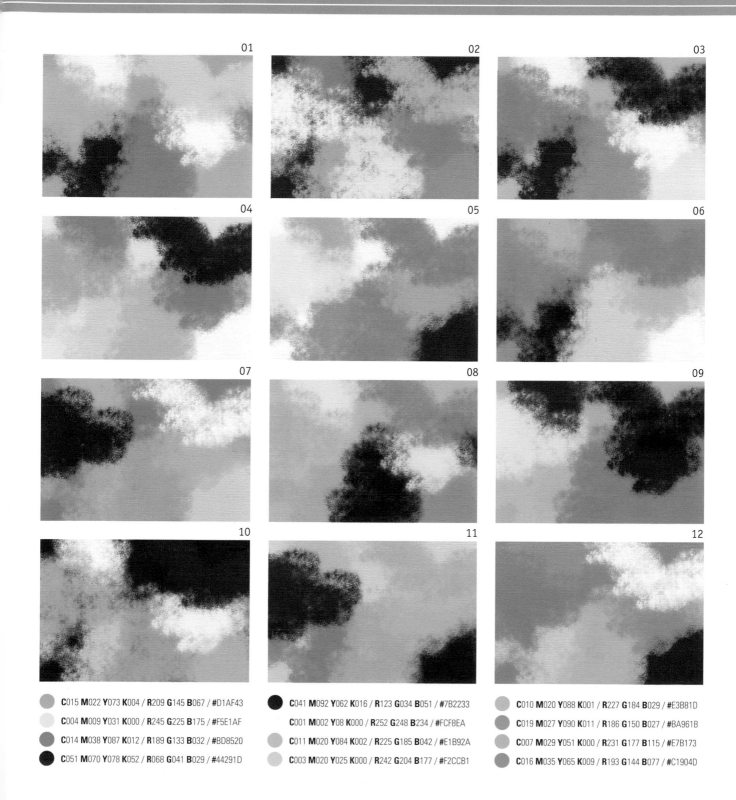

C015 M022 Y073 K004 / R209 G145 B067 / #D1AF43

C004 M009 Y031 K000 / R245 G225 B175 / #F5E1AF

C014 M038 Y087 K012 / R189 G133 B032 / #BD8520

C051 M070 Y078 K052 / R068 G041 B029 / #44291D

C041 M092 Y062 K016 / R123 G034 B051 / #7B2233

C001 M002 Y08 K000 / R252 G248 B234 / #FCF8EA

C011 M020 Y084 K002 / R225 G185 B042 / #E1B92A

C003 M020 Y025 K000 / R242 G204 B177 / #F2CCB1

C010 M020 Y088 K001 / R227 G184 B029 / #E3B81D

C019 M027 Y090 K011 / R186 G150 B027 / #BA961B

C007 M029 Y051 K000 / R231 G177 B115 / #E7B173

C016 M035 Y065 K009 / R193 G144 B077 / #C1904D

01

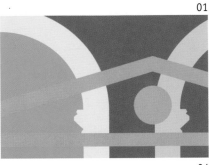

02

03

04

05

06

07

08

09

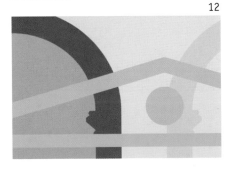

10

11

12

C043 M042 Y063 K011 / R133 G115 B076 / #85734C

C011 M009 Y027 K000 / R229 G220 B183 / #E5DCB7

C004 M007 Y020 K000 / R245 G231 B201 / #F5E7C9

C058 M002 Y031 K000 / R098 G178 B170 / #62B2AA

C044 M004 Y017 K000 / R140 G196 B201 / #8CC4C9

C042 M049 Y077 K020 / R123 G094 B049 / #7B5E31

C018 M013 Y017 K000 / R207 G206 B198 / #CFCEC6

C039 M039 Y045 K003 / R150 G132 B113 / #968471

C025 M026 Y044 K000 / R189 G170 B130 / #BDAA82

C002 M007 Y009 K000 / R248 G236 B226 / #F8ECE2

C018 M028 Y036 K000 / R205 G174 B145 / #CDAE91

C006 M012 Y016 K000 / R237 G220 B203 / #EDDCCB

01

02

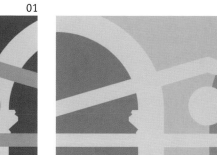

03

04

05

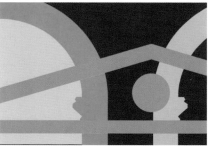

06

07

08

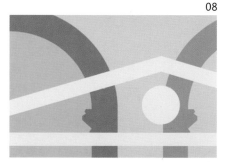

09

10

11

12

C048 **M**063 **Y**042 **K**011 / **R**120 **G**081 **B**092 / #98515C

C014 **M**027 **Y**009 **K**000 / **R**214 **G**184 **B**198 / #D6B8C6

C013 **M**020 **Y**004 **K**000 / **R**216 **G**199 **B**216 / #D8C7D8

C002 **M**050 **Y**058 **K**000 / **R**230 **G**133 **B**086 / #E685556

C004 **M**031 **Y**044 **K**000 / **R**236 **G**176 **B**128 / #ECB080

C062 **M**077 **Y**042 **K**020 / **R**086 **G**051 **B**074 / #56334A

C013 **M**018 **Y**018 **K**000 / **R**218 **G**200 **B**192 / #DAC8C0

C041 **M**045 **Y**039 **K**003 / **R**145 **G**121 **B**118 / #917976

C033 **M**044 **Y**025 **K**000 / **R**168 **G**133 **B**145 / #A88591

C009 **M**009 **Y**002 **K**000 / **R**230 **G**227 **B**236 / #E6E3EC

C034 **M**036 **Y**018 **K**000 / **R**165 **G**148 **B**166 / #A594A6

C016 **M**016 **Y**006 **K**000 / **R**212 **G**204 **B**216 / #D4CCD8

01

02

03

04

05

06

07

08

09

10

11

12

● C032 M078 Y100 K033 / R115 G047 B019 / #732F13

● C023 M033 Y059 K001 / R194 G157 B095 / #C29D5F

● C023 M091 Y086 K015 / R153 G035 B032 / #992320

● C025 M042 Y092 K004 / R182 G129 B028 / #B6811C

● C020 M030 Y064 K001 / R200 G162 B086 / #C8A256

● C013 M016 Y043 K000 / R223 G200 B142 / #DFC88E

● C044 M065 Y082 K045 / R085 G051 B031 / #55331F

● C037 M044 Y062 K009 / R148 G116 B079 / #94744F

● C018 M045 Y087 K002 / R199 G130 B037 / #C78225

● C026 M062 Y100 K013 / R158 G085 B016 / #9E5510

● C017 M068 Y053 K001 / R193 G087 B081 / #C15751

● C018 M057 Y075 K003 / R191 G106 B055 / #BF6A37

01

02

03

04

05

06

07

08

09

10

11

12

C065 M083 Y100 K033 / R069 G039 B022 / #452716

C016 M036 Y072 K001 / R209 G153 B067 / #D19943

C059 M090 Y100 K015 / R095 G039 B025 / #5F2719

C015 M057 Y099 K004 / R196 G105 B008 / #C46908

C013 M036 Y075 K001 / R214 G154 B061 / #D69A3D

C008 M019 Y053 K000 / R233 G197 B118 / #E9C576

C049 M065 Y093 K045 / R079 G051 B023 / #4F3317

C029 M043 Y074 K009 / R164 G121 B059 / #A4793B

C018 M057 Y099 K002 / R195 G106 B011 / #C36A0B

C041 M071 Y100 K013 / R131 G067 B022 / #834316

C030 M065 Y078 K001 / R169 G089 B050 / #A95932

C041 M058 Y089 K003 / R145 G095 B038 / #915F36

C038 **M**045 **Y**000 **K**000 / **R**152 **G**132 **B**183 / #9884B7

C017 **M**023 **Y**001 **K**000 / **R**206 **G**191 **B**218 / #CEBFDA

C040 **M**014 **Y**000 **K**010 / **R**150 **G**185 **B**205 / #96B9CD

C005 **M**013 **Y**024 **K**000 / **R**239 **G**218 **B**188 / #EFDABC

C029 **M**035 **Y**000 **K**000 / **R**175 **G**157 **B**199 / #AF9DC7

C013 **M**009 **Y**003 **K**000 / **R**220 **G**223 **B**223 / #DCDFE9

C007 **M**021 **Y**036 **K**000 / **R**234 **G**198 **B**153 / #EAC699

C027 **M**038 **Y**082 **K**003 / **R**180 **G**137 **B**049 / #B48931

C034 **M**062 **Y**005 **K**000 / **R**162 **G**099 **B**151 / #A26397

C009 **M**011 **Y**002 **K**000 / **R**230 **G**223 **B**223 / #E6DFE9

C015 **M**032 **Y**068 **K**000 / **R**213 **G**163 **B**077 / #D5A34D

C062 **M**029 **Y**020 **K**000 / **R**090 **G**138 **B**165 / #5A8AA5

01   02   03

04   05   06

07   08   09

10   11   12

C017 **M**044 **Y**024 **K**009 / **R**186 **G**132 **B**138 / #BA848A

C005 **M**024 **Y**014 **K**006 / **R**220 **G**186 **B**185 / #DCBAB9

C042 **M**000 **Y**033 **K**011 / **R**133 **G**180 **B**155 / #85B49B

C004 **M**013 **Y**018 **K**003 / **R**236 **G**215 **B**196 / #ECD7C4

C013 **M**035 **Y**020 **K**007 / **R**200 **G**156 **B**158 / #C89C9E

C011 **M**005 **Y**014 **K**006 / **R**215 **G**218 **B**204 / #D7DACC

C002 **M**022 **Y**023 **K**002 / **R**238 **G**197 **B**176 / #EEC5B0

C025 **M**031 **Y**051 **K**007 / **R**178 **G**150 **B**106 / #B2966A

C001 **M**071 **Y**022 **K**006 / **R**210 **G**084 **B**114 / #D25472

C004 **M**011 **Y**011 **K**005 / **R**233 **G**217 **B**208 / #E9D9D0

C012 **M**030 **Y**040 **K**002 / **R**215 **G**171 **B**135 / #D7AB87

C061 **M**006 **Y**048 **K**015 / **R**082 **G**145 **B**115 / #529173

01
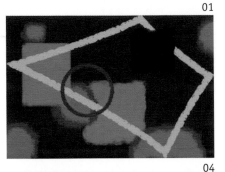

02
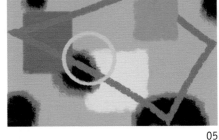

03
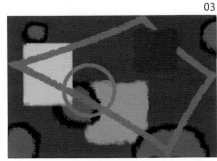

04
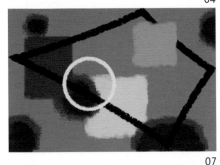

05

06
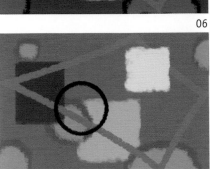

07
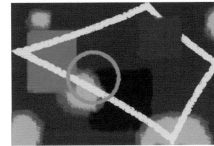

08

09
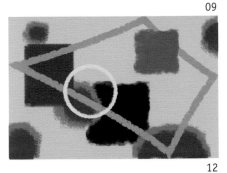

10
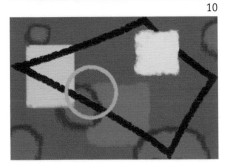

11
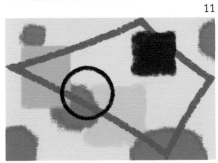

12
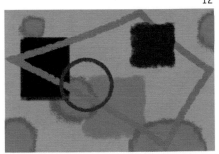

C084 M083 Y036 K027 / R044 G040 B071 / #2C2847

C043 M041 Y068 K011 / R132 G114 B069 / #847245

C082 M078 Y050 K058 / R030 G029 B040 / #1E1D28

C044 M063 Y035 K007 / R133 G086 B103 / #855667

C023 M026 Y044 K000 / R195 G172 B131 / #C3AC83

C016 M060 Y065 K02 / R195 G104 B069 / #C36845

C045 M083 Y040 K016 / R118 G047 B075 / #762F4B

C012 M012 Y003 K000 / R223 G218 B230 / #DFDAE6

C072 M071 Y033 K015 / R069 G059 B090 / #453B5A

C055 M052 Y025 K002 / R113 G103 B131 / #716783

C019 M014 Y055 K000 / R209 G196 B116 / #D1C474

C015 M044 Y054 K000 / R209 G142 B098 / #D18E62

01
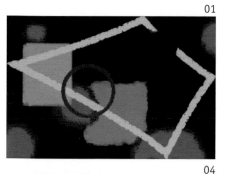

02
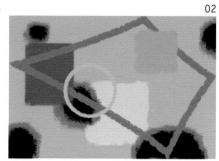

03
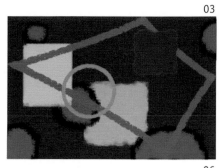

04
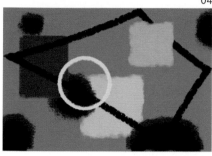

05

06
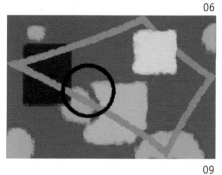

07
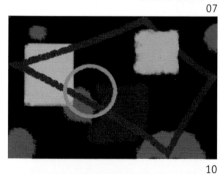

08
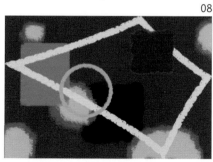

09

10
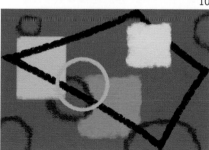

11
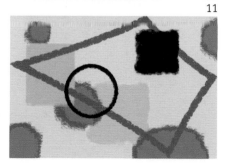

12
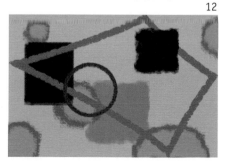

C088 M100 Y022 K010 / R047 G028 B085 / #2F1C55

C047 M038 Y059 K009 / R126 G121 B086 / #7E7956

C084 M089 Y042 K043 / R037 G029 B053 / #251D35

C035 M067 Y045 K009 / R147 G080 B086 / #935056

C022 M019 Y038 K000 / R198 G188 B150 / #C6BC96

C013 M047 Y078 K001 / R210 G132 B053 / #D28435

C029 M090 Y066 K022 / R134 G034 B045 / #86222D

C011 M018 Y000 K000 / R223 G208 B228 / #DFD0E4

C074 M087 Y016 K003 / R076 G045 B104 / #4C2D68

C056 M066 Y011 K001 / R113 G081 B134 / #715186

C024 M014 Y041 K000 / R195 G194 B146 / #C3C292

C011 M030 Y060 K000 / R221 G171 B096 / #DDAB60

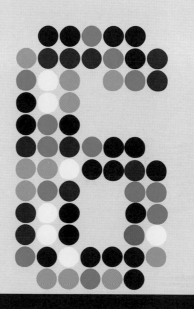

Color System
Palettes

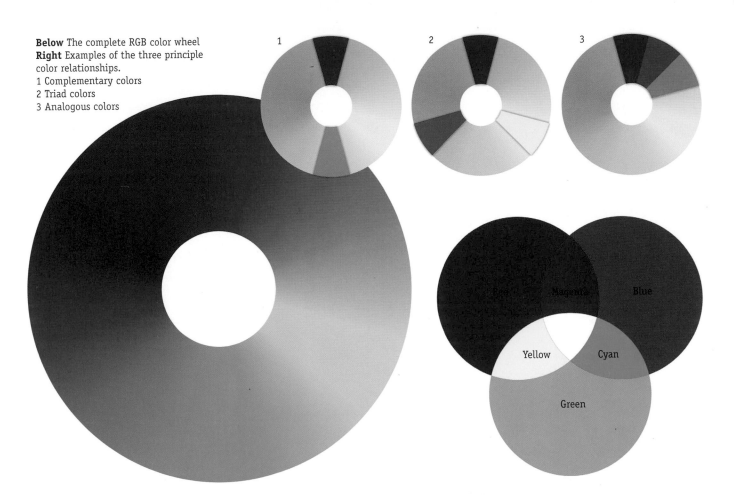

Below The complete RGB color wheel
Right Examples of the three principle color relationships.
1 Complementary colors
2 Triad colors
3 Analogous colors

The palettes on the previous pages are not the result of any color theory, or constrained by any systematic approach. However, it is possible to create palettes based on specific color relationships and the following pages demonstrate some of these.

Color is confined to the visible spectrum, the colors of the rainbow, that we generally refer to as red, orange, yellow, green, blue, indigo, violet, and all the shades between. There are various components that describe any color. Saturation is the purity of a hue. Intensity is the brightness or dullness of a hue. Luminance is the amount of light reflected from a hue. Chroma is how pure a hue is in relation to gray.

The color wheel is a common device used to show the RGB color spectrum and it can be used to demonstrate certain color relationships. For example, complementary colors are those that are opposite each other on the wheel, analogous colors are adjacent to each other, and triad are three colors that are equidistant from each other.

RGB is known as "additive" because when red, green, and blue are combined the result is white. When these three colors overlap they create cyan, magenta, yellow, and white. This is the color space used by monitors and TVs.

CMY is known as "subtractive" because when cyan, magenta, and yellow pigments are combined they should produce black (subtracting from white). However in the real world of ink printed on paper, to achieve the dense black that is required for the reproduction of many images, the mid and lighter tones invariably looked muddy, so a fourth color was added and that was black. To avoid any confusion with the blue of RGB and because the black provided a key for the other colors it is referred to as K—hence CMYK, the four process colors used for the majority of printing.

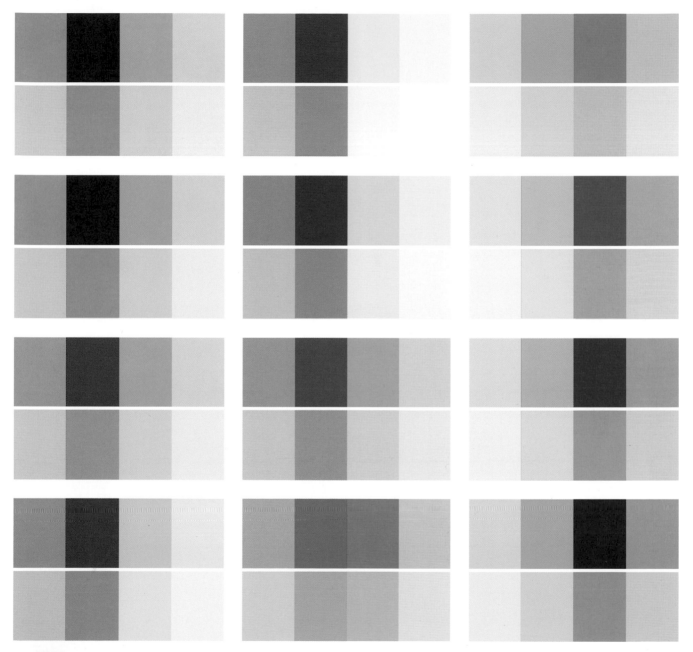

This is the start position for this sequence of complementary colors. The other templates have been created by rotating the arrow in a counterclockwise direction. Lighter shades of the start colors are also shown.

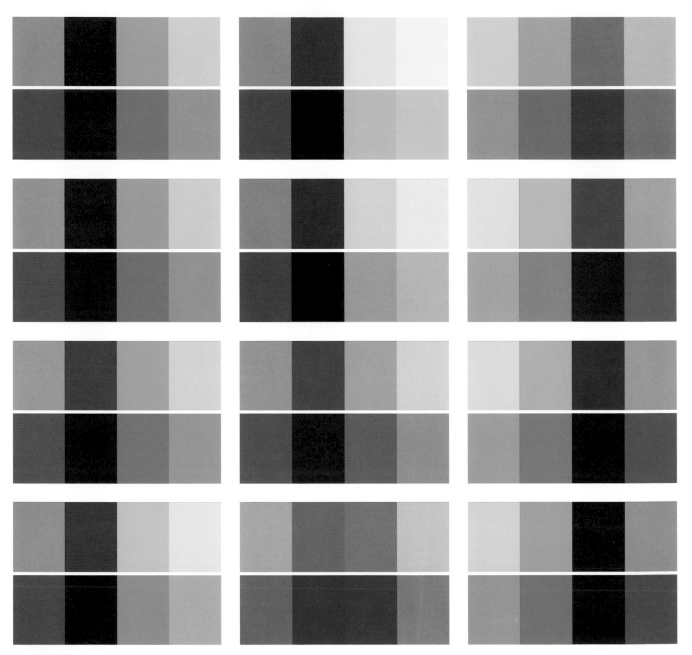

This is the start position for this sequence of complementary colors. The other templates have been created by rotating the arrows in a counterclockwise direction. Darker shades of the start colors are also shown.

This is the start position for this sequence of triad colors. The other templates have been created by rotating the arrows in a counterclockwise direction. Lighter shades of the start colors are also shown.

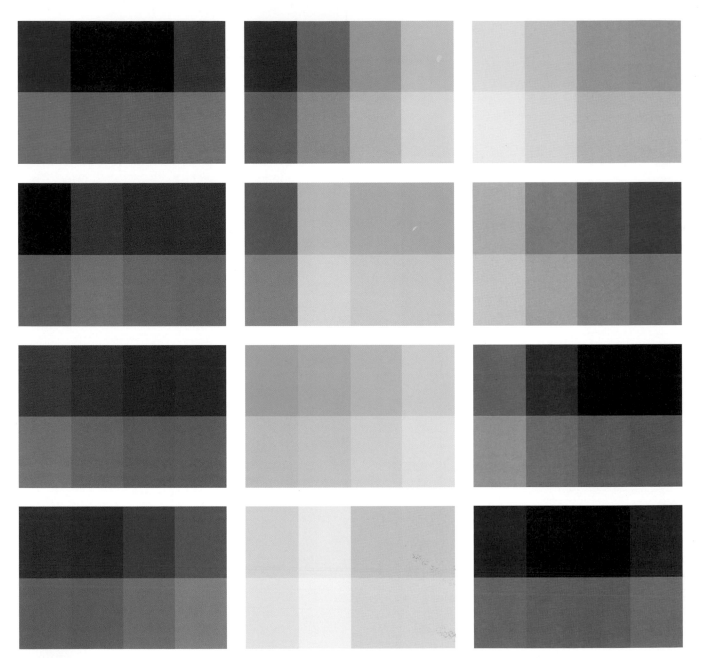

This is the start position for this sequence of analogous colors. The other templates have been created by rotating the arrows in a counterclockwise direction. Lighter shades of the start colors are also shown.

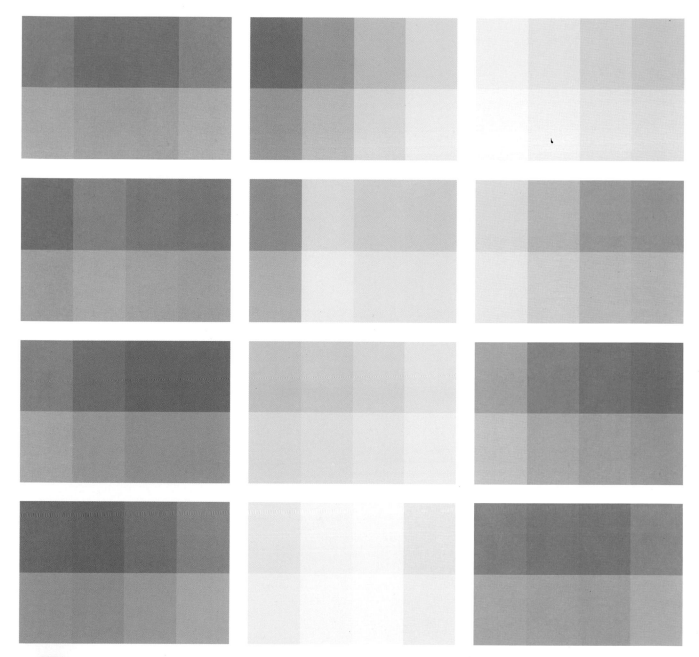

This is the start position for this sequence of analogous colors. They are the same colors as those opposite but with lower intensity. The other templates have been created by rotating the arrows in a counterclockwise direction.

Reference

Glossary

additive color mixing The mixing of red, green, and blue light (with all at equal strength) to create white light, or any other color by using different strengths. The basis of all screen display and digital image capturing.

analogous scheme A color scheme that uses two or more colors that would sit adjacent to each other in a color wheel.

antialiasing The insertion of pixels of various shades into a bitmapped graphic to smooth out "jagged" transitions between contrasting tones, for example along a diagonal line.

baseline An imaginary line that characters rest on in a line of text.

baseline grid A horizontal grid used to align text and graphic elements in graphics and desktop publishing applications.

Bézier tools Vector-based drawing tools, employed by most graphics programs. A pen tool allows a user to place a series of points on the page. The points are automatically joined by a line, with two "handles" on each point controlling the curve of the line.

bit A contraction of "binary digit," the smallest unit of information that a computer can use. A bit may have one of two values: on or off, 1 or 0. Eight bits form a byte.

bitmap An image composed of dots, such as a digital photo. A bitmap is a table of values corresponding to the pixels that make up the image. "Bitmap fonts," for example, contain such an image of each character, with each pixel represented by one bit that can be either black or white. Color images typically use at least 24 bits (3 bytes) for each pixel, allowing millions of colors to be represented. The finite number of pixels in a bitmap limits the maximum size at which it can be reproduced at acceptable visual quality, unlike vector graphics.

bleed The margin outside the trimmed area of a sheet that allows for tints, images, and other matter to print beyond the edge of the page. For printing without bleed, the designer must leave a blank margin around the page.

body text The matter that forms the main text of a printed book, excluding captions, headings, page numbers, and so on.

box model A method of defining the positioning of elements within a CSS based Web page.

broadband Used to describe any telecom link with a high bandwidth, enabling a fast rate of data flow. Specifically, a digital Internet connection made via ADSL or cable modem.

browser An application that enables the user to view (or "browse") Web pages across the Internet. The most widely used browsers are Netscape Navigator and Microsoft Internet Explorer. Version numbers are particularly important in the use of browsers because they indicate the level of HTML that can be supported.

CAD Acronym for "computer-aided design." May refer to any design carried out using a computer, but usually to three-dimensional design, such as product design or architecture. Software may control the entire process from concept to finished product, sometimes termed CAD-CAM (computer-aided manufacturing).

caption Strictly speaking, a caption is a headline printed above an illustration, identifying the contents of the image. However, the word is now used to describe any descriptive text that accompanies illustrative matter, usually set below or beside it at a small size. Not to be confused with "credit," the small print beside a picture that identifies the illustrator, photographer, or copyright holder.

CD-ROM Acronym for "compact disk, read-only memory." A CD-based method for the storage and distribution of digital data. Based on audio CD technology, CD-ROMs can store up to 800 megabytes of data, and are available in record-once (CD-R) or rewritable (CD-RW) formats.

cell A rectangle that occurs when rows and columns within a table intersect.

character A letter of the alphabet, numeral or typographic symbol. The table of contents of a font is its character set, which may include more than those shown on the keyboard.

chroma The intensity or purity of a color, and so its degree of saturation. Technically it refers to the mixture of wavelengths in a light source, where a single wavelength is the maximum chroma and an even mixture of all wavelengths is the minimum.

CMYK An abbreviation for cyan, magenta, yellow, and black (black being denoted by "K" for "key plate") in four-color process printing.

color The Visible spectrum (i.e. the colors of the rainbow that we generally refer to as red, orange, yellow, green, blue, indigo, and violet—and all the shades between).

ColorSync Apple's color management system, an implementation of the ICC system.

color constancy The ability of the human eye and brain to perceive colors accurately under a variety of lighting conditions, compensating automatically for the difference in color temperature. This phenomenon is also known as chromatic adaption.

color management The process of controlling the representation and conversion of color information. The designer's computer should have a color management system (CMS) such as ColorSync, which is used by software to help ensure colors appear consistently across all devices, including the monitor.

color space A description of the full range of colors that can be output or displayed by any single reproduction device (monitor, printer, etc.), including any tonal and color variations.

color wheel A circular diagram representing the complete spectrum of visible colors.

complementary scheme A color scheme using two similar colors.

compression The technique of rearranging data so that it either occupies less space on disk, or transfers more quickly between devices or along communication lines. Different kinds of compression are used for different kinds of data. Software applications, for example, must not lose any data when compressed, whereas images, sound, and movies can tolerate a large amount of data loss.

contrast The degree of difference between tones in an image from the lightest to the darkest. "High contrast" describes an image with light highlights and dark shadows, whereas a "low contrast" image is one with more even tones and few extreme dark areas or light highlights.

corporate identity A design or set of designs for use on corporate stationery, livery, etc.

CSS Abbreviation for "cascading style sheets." These extend the capabilities of HTML, allowing the Web designer to exercise detailed control over layout and typography, applying preset formats to paragraphs, page elements, or entire pages. Several style sheets can be applied to a single page, thus "cascading." Correct use of CSS helps create pages that display as intended in all browsers.

default settings The settings of a hardware device or software program that are determined at the time of manufacture. These settings remain in effect until the user changes them; such changes will be stored in a "preferences" file. Default settings are otherwise known as "factory" settings.

digital press A printing press that outputs pages directly from digital files, typically using some form of inkjet technology.

DHTML Dynamic HTML, extensions that enable a Web page to respond to user input.

display type Text set in large-size fonts for headings, or any matter that is intended to stand out. Fonts too ornate for general text, or specially designed for larger sizes, are referred to as display faces.

div The <div> tag defines a division or section in a Web page.

document A file produced using a graphics or desktop publishing application.

dpi Abbreviation for "dots per inch." A unit of measurement used to represent the resolution of devices such as printers and imagesetters. The more dots, the better the quality. Typical values include 300dpi for a laser printer, and 2450dpi+ for an imagesetter. Dots per inch is sometimes erroneously used as a value when discussing monitors or images; the correct unit in these cases is ppi (pixels per inch).

Dreamweaver Adobe's leading Web design tool.

DVD Abbreviation for "digital versatile (or video) disk." Similar to a CD-ROM , but distinguished by its greater capacity (up to 9 gigabytes).

embedded fonts Fonts that are fixed within files, meaning that the original font folder does not need to be provided in order for the file to be printed or set.

EPS Abbreviation for "encapsulated PostScript." A graphics file format used primarily for storing object-oriented or vector graphics. An EPS file consists of two parts: PostScript code that tells the printer how to print the image; and an onscreen preview, that usually saved alongside in JPEG, TIFF, or PICT format.

float A CSS property that defines where an image or block of text will appear in another element.

font A complete set of type characters of the same size, style, and design.

format In printing, the size or orientation of a book or page.

four-color process Any printing process that reproduces full-color images that have been separated into three basic "process" colors—cyan, magenta, and yellow—with a fourth color, black, added for greater contrast. *See also* CMYK.

frame (1) In page-layout software, a container for text or image.

frame (2) On the Web, a means of splitting a page into several areas that can be updated separately. This was a popular way of laying out pages before cascading style sheets (CSS).

FTP File Transfer Protocol. A method of transferring files from one computer to another via the Internet.

GIF Acronym for "graphic interchange format." A bitmapped graphics format that compresses data without losing any information, as opposed to JPEG, which discards data selectively.

glyph A letter, number, or symbol in a particular typeface, referring to its visual appearance rather than its function. Any number of alternative glyphs may represent the same character.

graphic A general term used to describe any illustration or drawn design. May also be used for a type design based on drawn letters.

grid A template—usually showing such things as column widths, picture areas, and trim sizes—used to design publications with multiple pages, to ensure the design remains consistent.

guides Non-printing aids to alignment.

gutter The space between columns on a layout.

hairline rule The thinnest line it is possible to print, with a width of 0.25pt.

halftone The technique of reproducing a continuous tone image, such as a photo, on a printing press by breaking it into equally spaced dots of varying sizes.

heading A title that appears either at the top of a chapter, or at the beginning of a subdivision within the body text.

hexadecimal A numeral system using letters and numbers to represent values in base 16. RGB color values are written with three hexadecimal pairs in the form #RRGGBB.

hinting In typography, information contained within outline fonts that modifies character shapes to enhance them when they are displayed or printed at low resolutions.

HSB Abbreviation for "hue, saturation, and brightness," to describe a color.

HTML Abbreviation for "hypertext mark-up language." A text-based page-description language used to format documents on the Web and viewed on Web browsers.

hue Pure spectral color that distinguishes one color from others. For example, red is a different hue to blue. Light red and dark red may vary in appearance, but they are the same hue.

hyperlink A contraction of "hypertext link," which is a link to other documents that is embedded within the original document. Clicking on a hyperlink will take the user to another document or Web site.

ICC The International Color Consortium that oversees the most widely used standards for color management systems.

Illustrator Adobe's Vector-based drawing software.

image map An image, usually on a Web page, that contains embedded links to other documents or Web sites. These links are activated when the appropriate area of the image is clicked on. Most image maps are now "client-side," stored within the page's HTML code rather than "server-side," accessed from a server.

imposition The arrangement of pages in the sequence and position in which they will appear on the printed sheet, with appropriate margins for folding and trimming, before printing.

InDesign Leading desktop publishing software from Adobe, and a rival to QuarkXPress.

indexed color A palette where the RGB color range is restricted to 8 bits making a maximum of 256 discreet colors available, usually used for Web-based images where a limited range of colors is acceptable.

inkjet printer A printing device that creates an image by spraying tiny jets of ink on to the paper surface at high speed.

Internet Explorer Web-browsing software produced by Microsoft.

intranet A network of computers similar to the Internet, to which the public does not have access. Mainly used by large corporations or governmental institutions.

ISO paper sizes The paper-size system, devised by the International Standards Organization, where the height to width (aspect) ratio is always 1.4142:1. If you put two such pages next to each other, the resulting page will have again the same width to height ratio.

ISP Abbreviation for "Internet service provider." Any organization that provides access to the Internet. Most ISPs also provide other services, such as e-mail addresses.

JavaScript Netscape's Java-like scripting language that provides a simplified method of adding dynamic effects to Web pages.

JPEG Abbreviation for "Joint Photographic Experts Group." This International Standards Organization group defines compression standards for bitmapped color images, and has given its name to a popular compressed file format. JPEG files are "lossy" (lose data during compression), but work in such a way as to minimize the visible effect on graduated tone images. Pronounced "jay-peg."

L*a*b A color model, created by the Commission Internationale de l'Eclairage (CIE), which is perceptually based. It was created through a series of experiments that required subjects to match sample colors. L is a luminance and A and B are color axes.

layers In some applications, a level to which the user can consign an element of the design being worked on. Individual layers can be active (meaning that they can be worked on), or non-active.

layout The placement of various elements—text, headings, images, etc.—on a printed page.

leading The spacing between lines of type.

Lock To A pseudomagnetic effect used to align elements to guides or grid in graphics and desktop publishing applications; Also known as *Snap To*. Elements may snap to a predefined grid, or to other objects already added to the design.

luminance In the L*a*b* color system, this refers to the brightness of a color, from solid black to the brightest possible value.

margins The space outside the text area of a page in graphics and desktop publishing applications, or a CSS property defining the space around elements contained in a Web page.

master page In some applications, a template that includes attributes that will be common to all pages, such as the number of text columns, page numbers, running heads, and so on.

metamerism A property of printer material where the gray balance appears to change in response to different lighting conditions. This is caused by different spectral qualities of light.

Nested Style Sheet A sequence of text formatting that is applied automatically to text.

OpenType A relatively new font format that can contain either PostScript or TrueType data and allows large numbers of characters in one file.

Padding The space between the element border and the element content within a table or CSS style sheet.

PageMaker The original page-layout software, now replaced by InDesign.

PANTONE The proprietary trademark for PANTONE's system of color standards, control, and quality requirements, in which each color bears a description of its formulation (in percentages) for subsequent printing.

PDF Abbreviation for "portable document format." A multipurpose format from Adobe that allows complex, multifeatured documents to be created, retaining all text, layout, and picture formatting, then to be viewed and printed on any computer with PDF "reader" software (such as the free Adobe Reader) or, if correctly formatted, used for final output on a printing press.

Photoshop Hugely powerful, industry-standard image manipulation software from Adobe. Also available as Photoshop Elements, which is a pared down version aimed at nonprofessional users.

pixel Contraction of "picture element." The smallest component of a digital image, such as a single dot of light on a computer monitor. In its most simple form, one pixel corresponds to a single bit : 0 = off (white); 1 = on (black). In color and grayscale images (or monitors), one pixel may correspond to several bits: an 8-bit pixel, for example, can be displayed in any of 256 colors (the total number of different configurations that can be achieved by eight 0s and 1s).

plug-in Software, usually developed by a third party, that extends the capabilities of another program. Plug-ins are common in image-editing and page-layout software for such things as special effects filters. They are also common in Web browsers for playing such things as movies and audio files.

point The basic unit of Anglo-American type measurement. There are 72 points to an inch.

PostScript Adobe's proprietary page description language for image output to laser printers and high-resolution imagesetters.

pre-press Any or all of the reproduction processes that occur between design and printing, especially color separation.

proof A prototype of a job (usually a printed document) produced to check quality and accuracy. An accurate on-screen preview of a job is known as a "soft proof".

QuarkXPress Industry standard page-layout program from Quark.

raster Deriving from the Latin *rastrum* (rake), a "raster image" is any image created as rows of pixels, dots, or lines in a "raking" sequence, i.e. from top to bottom of a page, monitor, etc. On a monitor, the screen image is made up from a pattern of several hundred parallel lines created by an electron beam that "rakes" the screen from top to bottom. The speed at which the image or frame is created is the "refresh" rate, quoted in hertz (Hz), equal to the number of times per second. Converting a vector image to a bitmap for output on screen or printer is "rasterization."

resolution The quantity of data points, such as pixels, with which an image, is stored digitally. Higher resolution means better definition, clarity, and fidelity, at the cost of larger files.

RGB Abbreviation for "red, green, blue." The primary colors of the "additive" color model, used in monitors and for Web and multimedia graphics.

RIP Acronym for "raster image processor." Used by a printer to convert and rasterize page-layout data, typically in a PostScript or PDF file, for printed output, as a proof, or on press.

sans serif The generic name for type designs that lack the small extensions (serifs) at the ends of the main strokes of the letters. Sometimes called "lineal type."

saturation The variation in color of the same tonal brightness from none (gray) through pastel shades (low saturation) to pure color with no gray (high or "full" saturation).

serif The short counterstroke or finishing stroke at the end of the main stroke of a type character.

Snap To A pseudomagnetic effect used to align elements in desktop publishing applications to a grid or guide.

Span The <span> tag is used to group inline elements in a document.

software The generic term that is used for any kind of computer application, as opposed to the physical hardware.

spot colors A printing color that has been specifically mixed for the job, as opposed to using the four-color process colors.

Style Sheet A group of formatting instructions that can be applied to individual characters or complete paragraphs.

Table A rectangle consisting of rows and columns, used to layout text in a Web or printed page.

tag Formatting commands in HTML and related mark-up languages. A tag is switched on by placing a command inside angle brackets ‹command› and turned off by the same command preceded with a forward slash ‹/command›.

template A document with pre-positioned areas, used as a basis for repeatedly creating others.

TIFF Acronym for "tagged image file format." A graphics file format used to store bitmapped images with no loss of data and optionally with extra features such as layers. Widely used in graphic design and pre-press.

tracking The adjustment of the spacing between characters in a piece of text.

trapping Settings in DTP (desktop publishing) programs that determine the interaction of overlapping colors. Also refers to printing problems when one solid color completely overprints another. Trapping preferences are complex and best left to the service bureau or printer.

triad Three colors equidistant from each other on the color wheel.

TrueType Apple Computer's digital font technology, developed as an alternative to PostScript and now used by both PCs and Macs. A single TrueType file is used for both printing and screen rendering, while PostScript fonts require two separate files.

Unicode A system used to identify which glyphs in a font represent which characters.

URL Abbreviation for "uniform resource locator." The unique address of any page on the Web, usually composed of three parts: protocol (such as "http"), domain name, and directory name.

vector A straight line segment of a given length and orientation. "Vector graphics"—which can involve more complex forms than straight lines, such as Bézier curves—are stored as numeric descriptions that can be scaled to reproduce the same visual result at any physical size, rather than broken up into discrete pixels as in the case of bitmapped images.

XHTML A combination of HTML and XML that is used to create Internet content for multiple devices.

XML An acronym for "extensible markup language" that is broader than HTML.

Useful Web sites

Newspaper Design
www.snd.org
www.newsdesigner.com
www.brasstacksdesign.com/design.htm
www.poynter.org/subject.asp?id=11
www.stbride.org

QuarkXPress & InDesign
www.quarkvsindesign.com
www.indesignusergroup.com
www.layersmagazine.com/indesign.html
www.indesignsecrets.com

International paper sizes
www.cl.cam.ac.uk/~mgk25/iso-paper.html

Design ref
www.designinteract.com/sow/archive.html
www.graphic-design.com

Fonts
www.1001freefonts.com
www.dafont.com
www.vlaurie.com/computers2/Articles/privchar.htm
www.home.kabelfoon.nl/~slam/fonts/truetypeviewer.html
www.creativepro.com/story/feature/17725.html

Web to print
www.princexml.com
www.alistapart.com/articles/boom
www.computerarts.co.uk/tutorials/new_media/
    magazine-style_layouts

Web CSS
www.accessat.c-net.us/articles/convert.html
www.builder.com.com/5100-6371-1049559.html
www.digital-web.com/articles/converting_a_page_to_css
www.adobe.com/products/dreamweaver/bestpractices/css
www.brainjar.com/css/positioning
www.dynamic-html-editor.com
www.inserit.com
www.oswd.org
www.openwebdesign.org
www.andreasviklund.com/templates
www.elliottback.com/wp/archives/2005/04/25/
    convert-image-to-css
www.theubergeeks.net/2004/04/22/css-in-a-timeframe

General ref
www.prepressure.com/library/wordoverview.htm
www.designtalkboard.com

Acknowledgments

This book would not have been possible without the unstinting support of my family and my dog Rufus, along with the professionalism and understanding of the editors at ILEX.